MAZES FOR KIDS

ACTIVITY COLORING BOOK

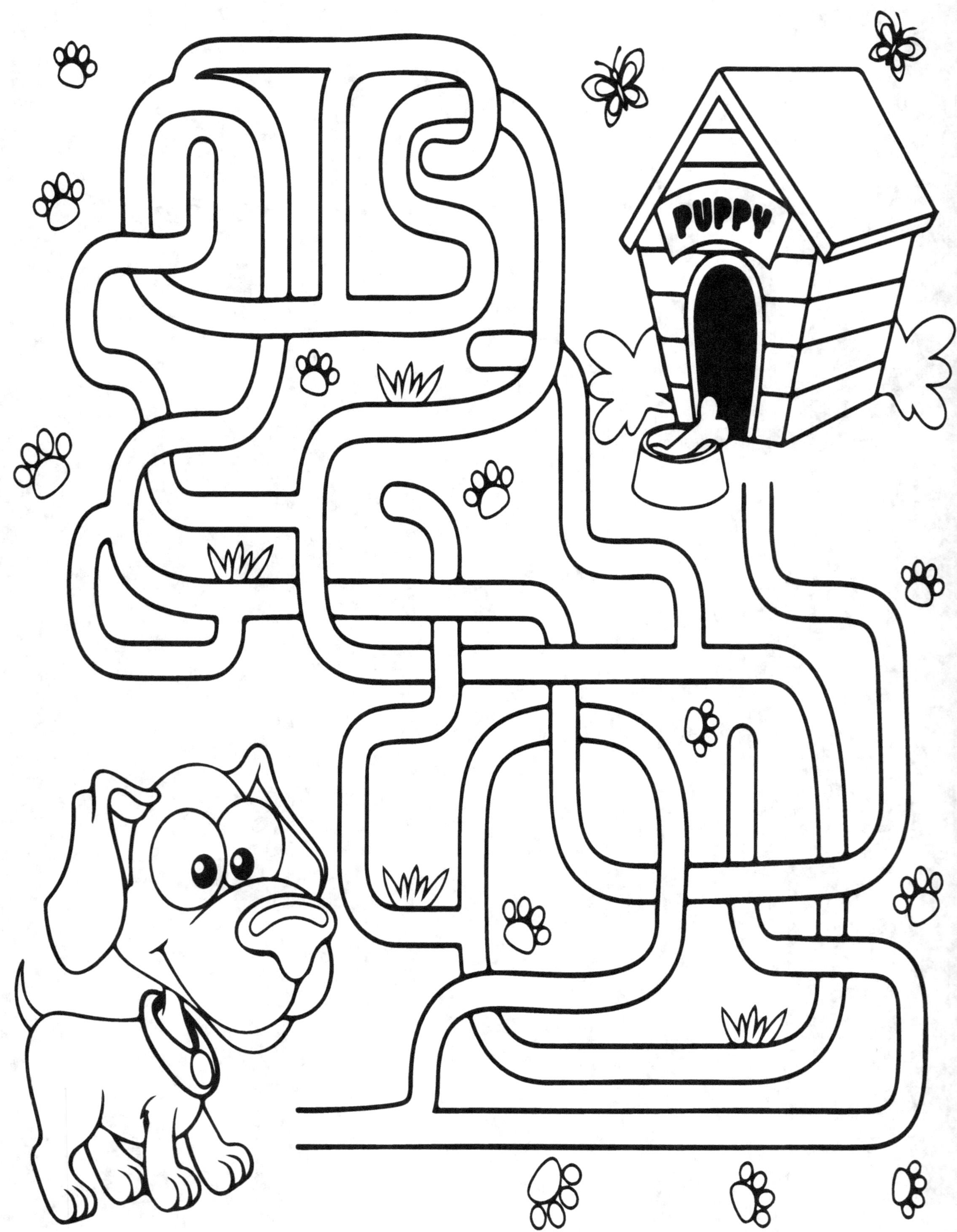

PUPPY

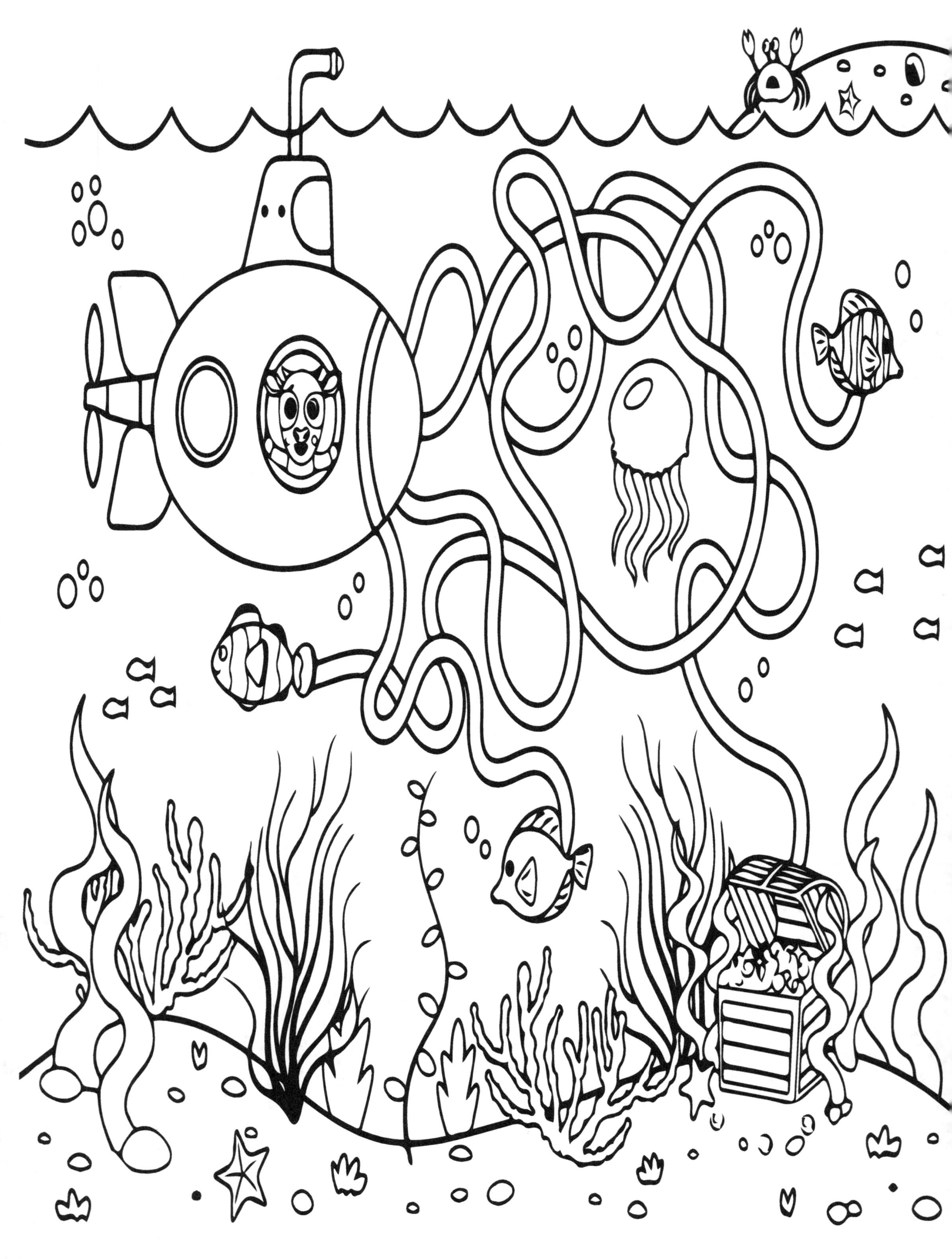

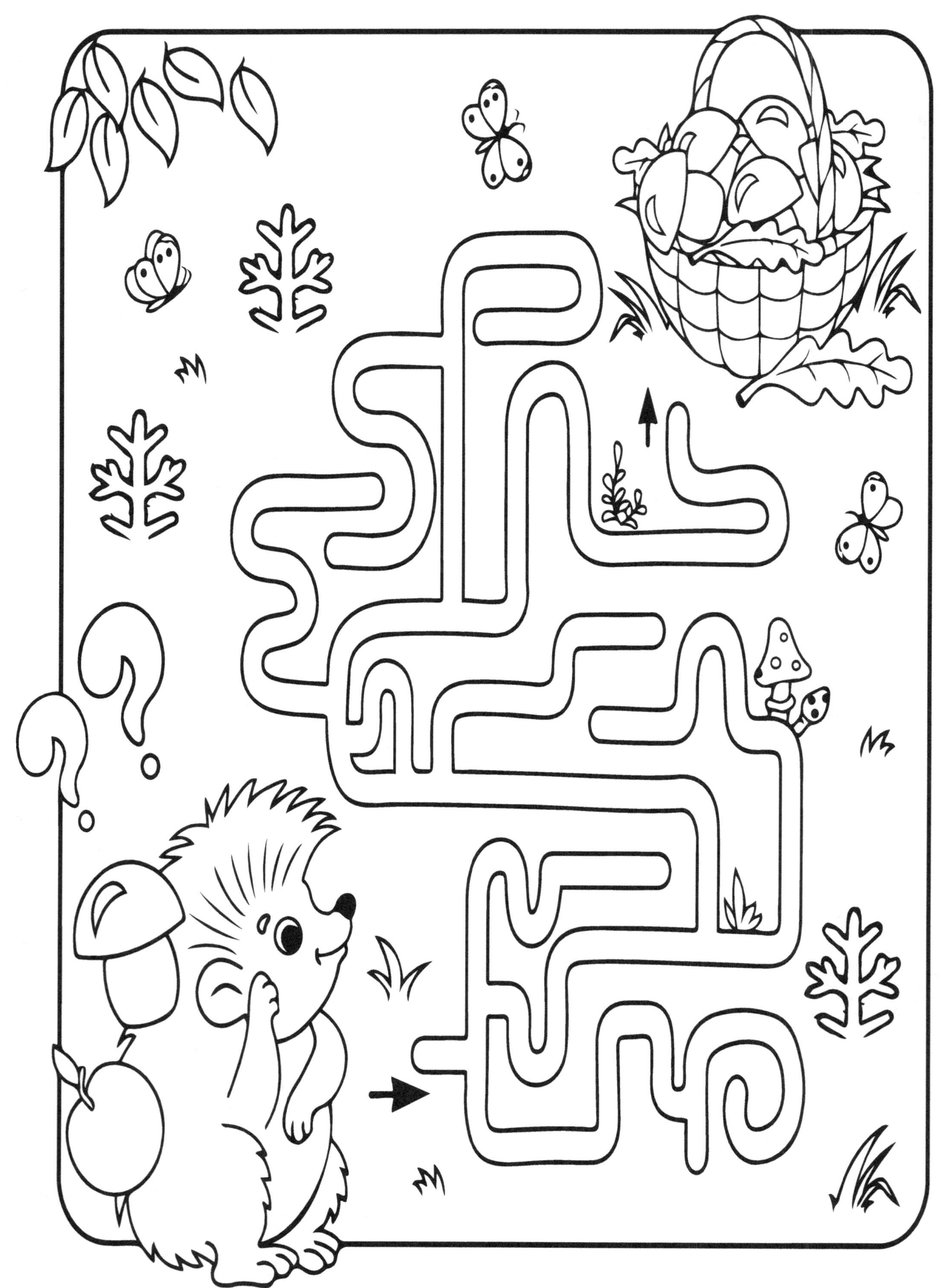

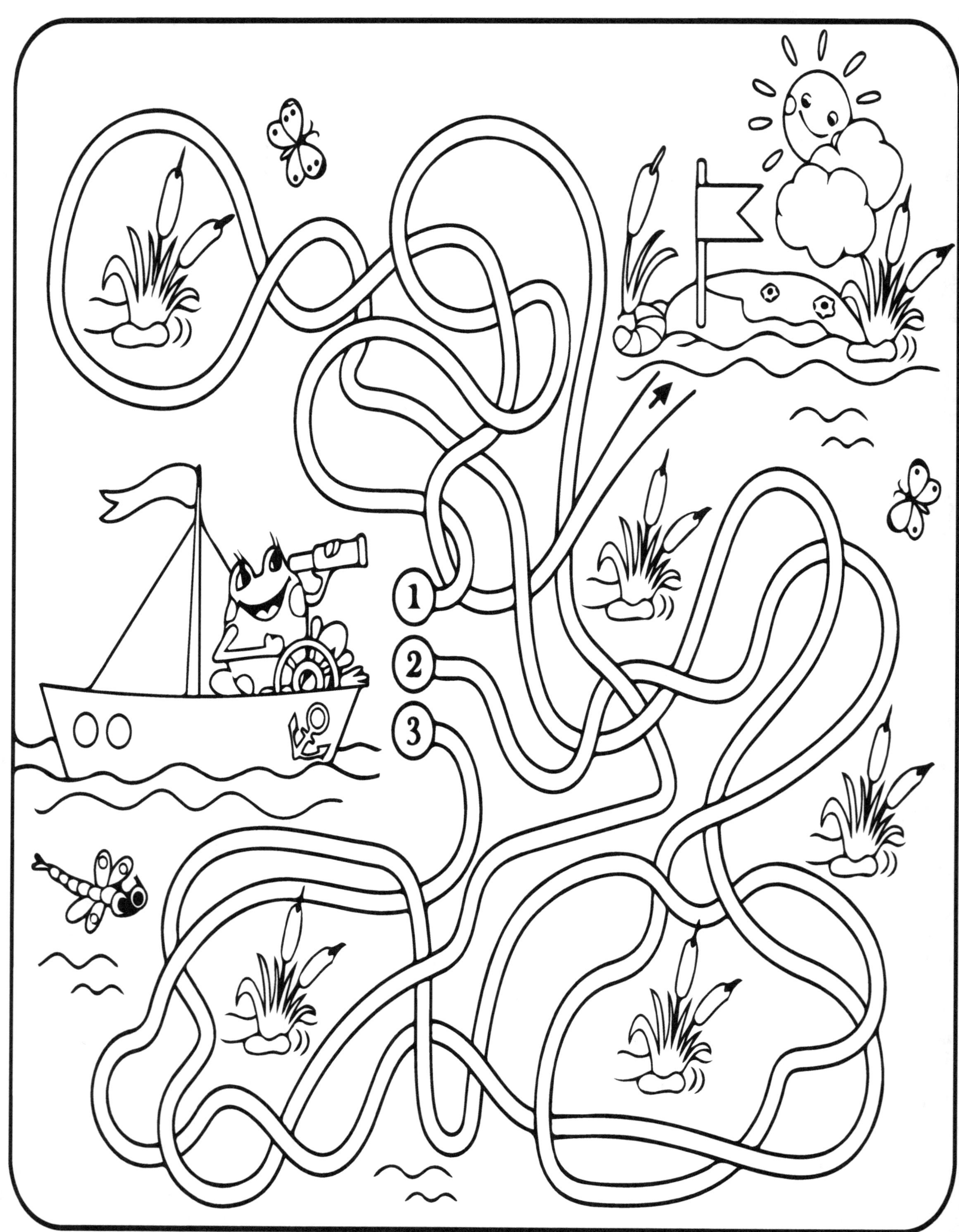

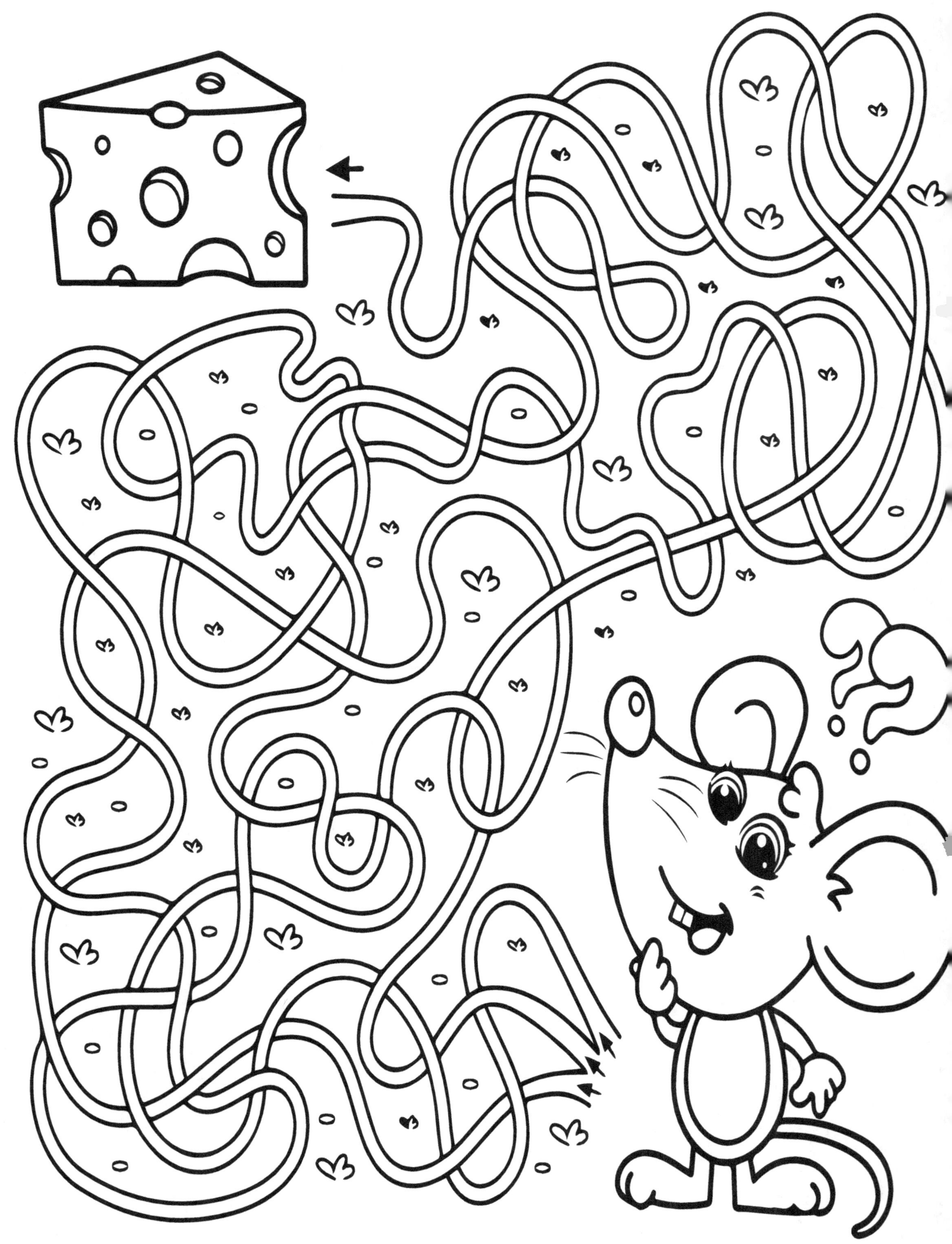

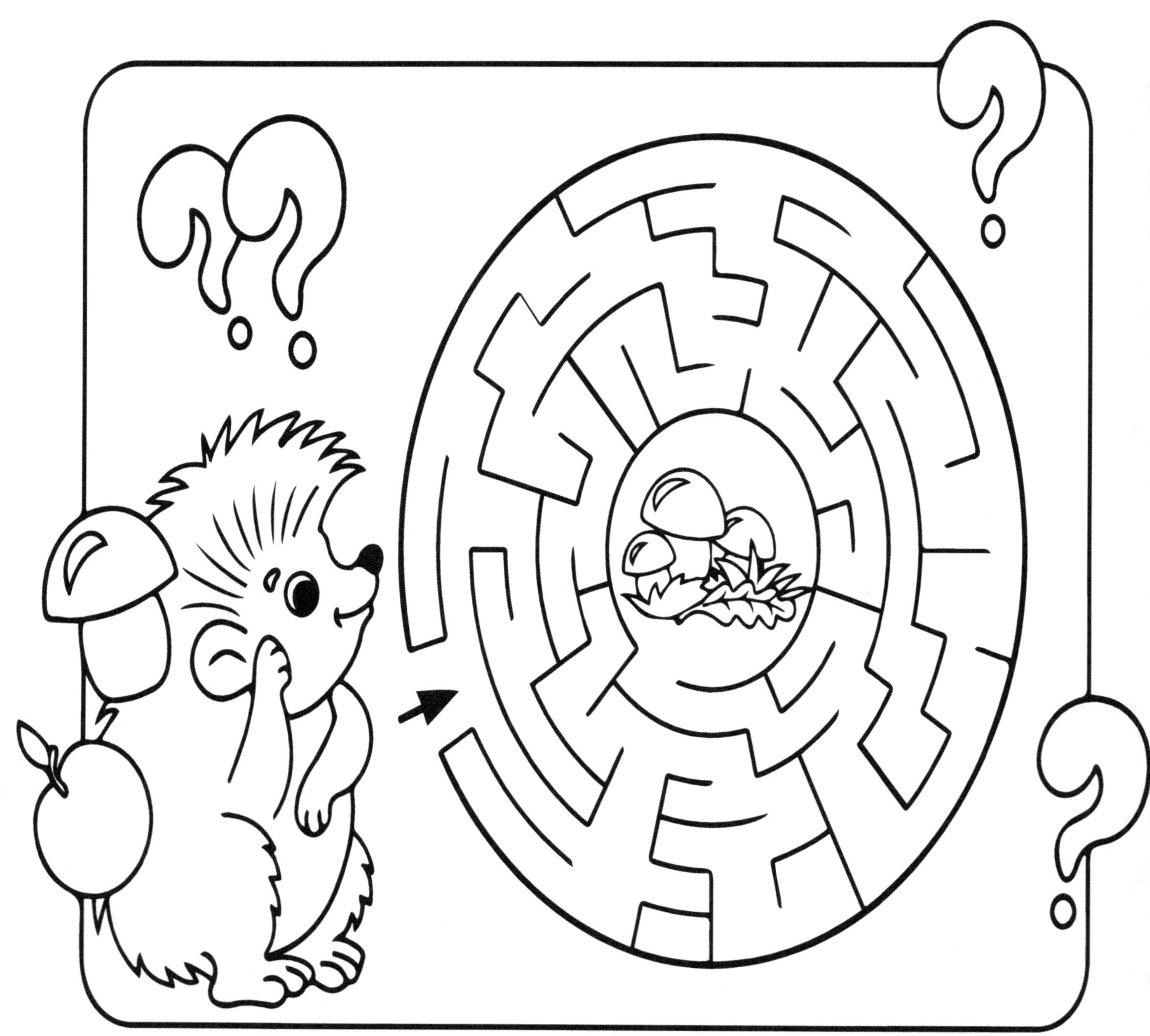

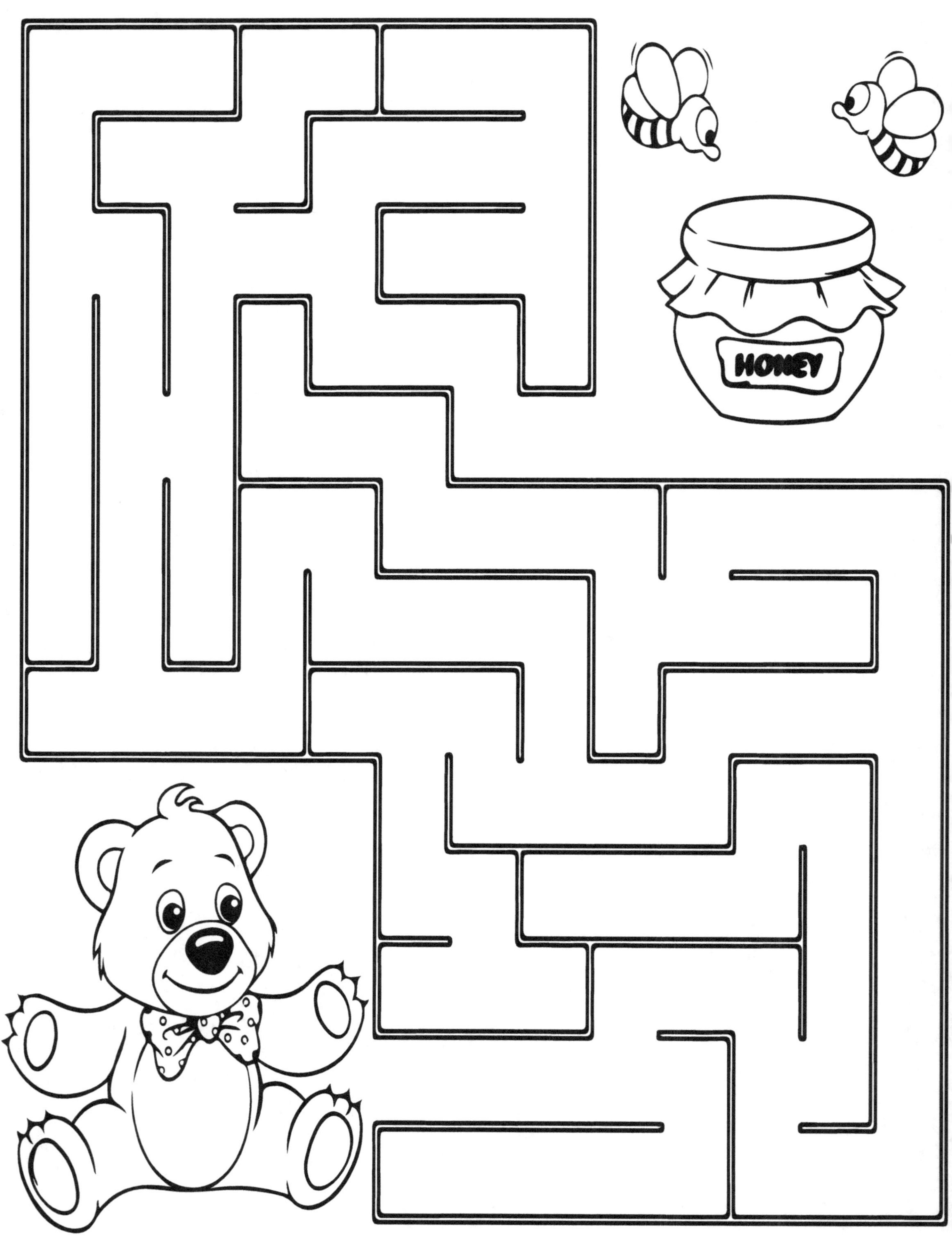
HONEY

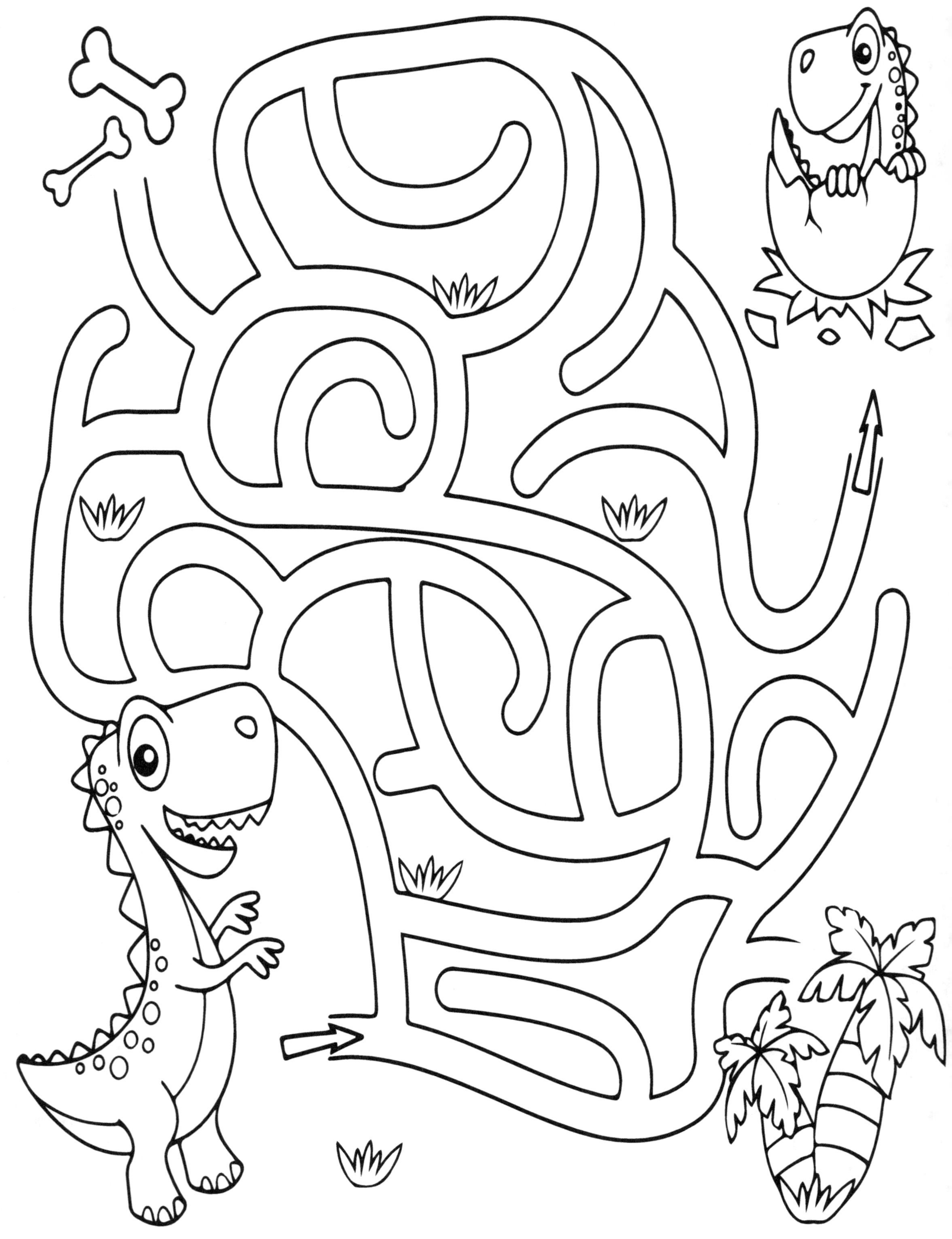

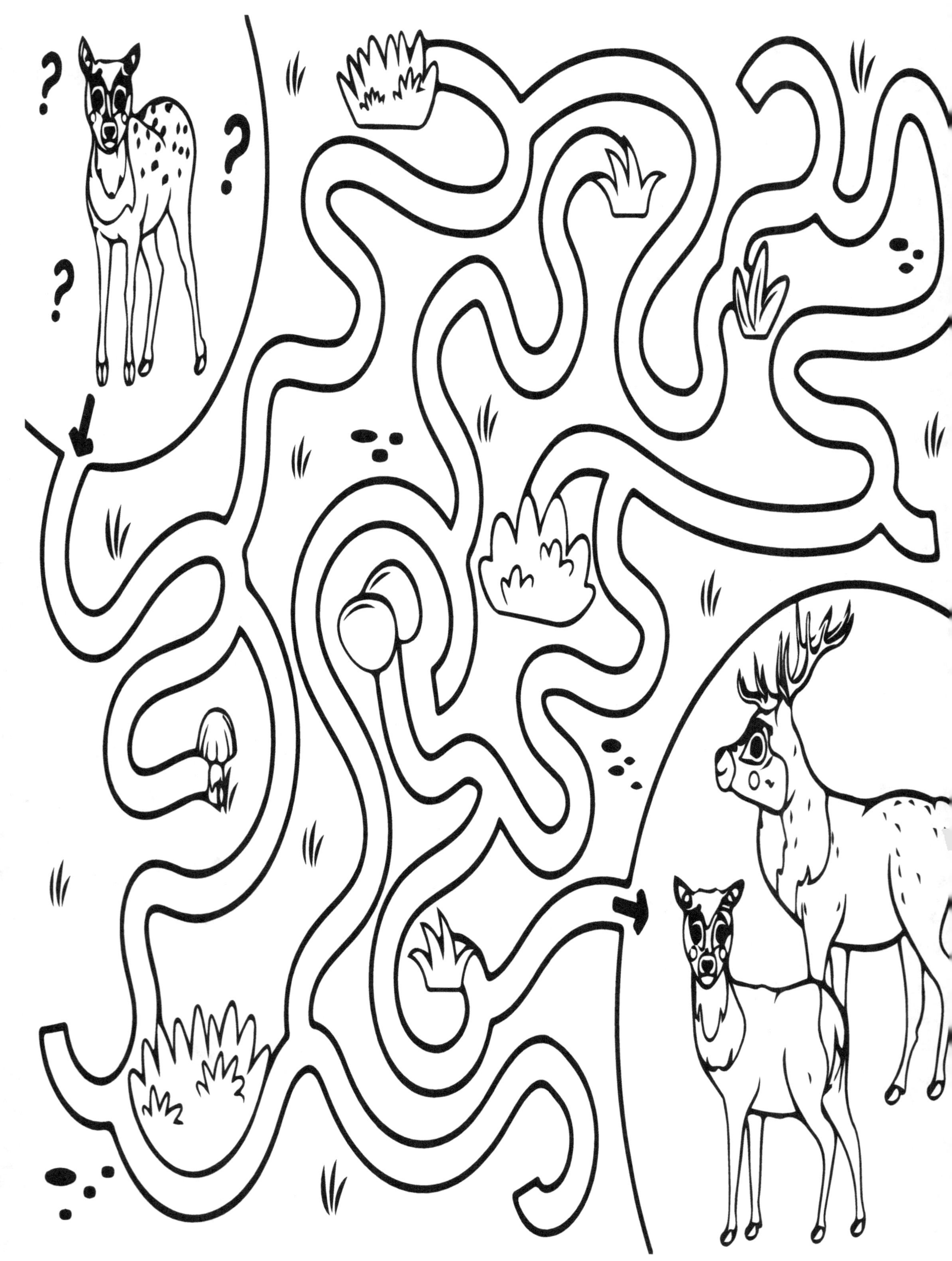

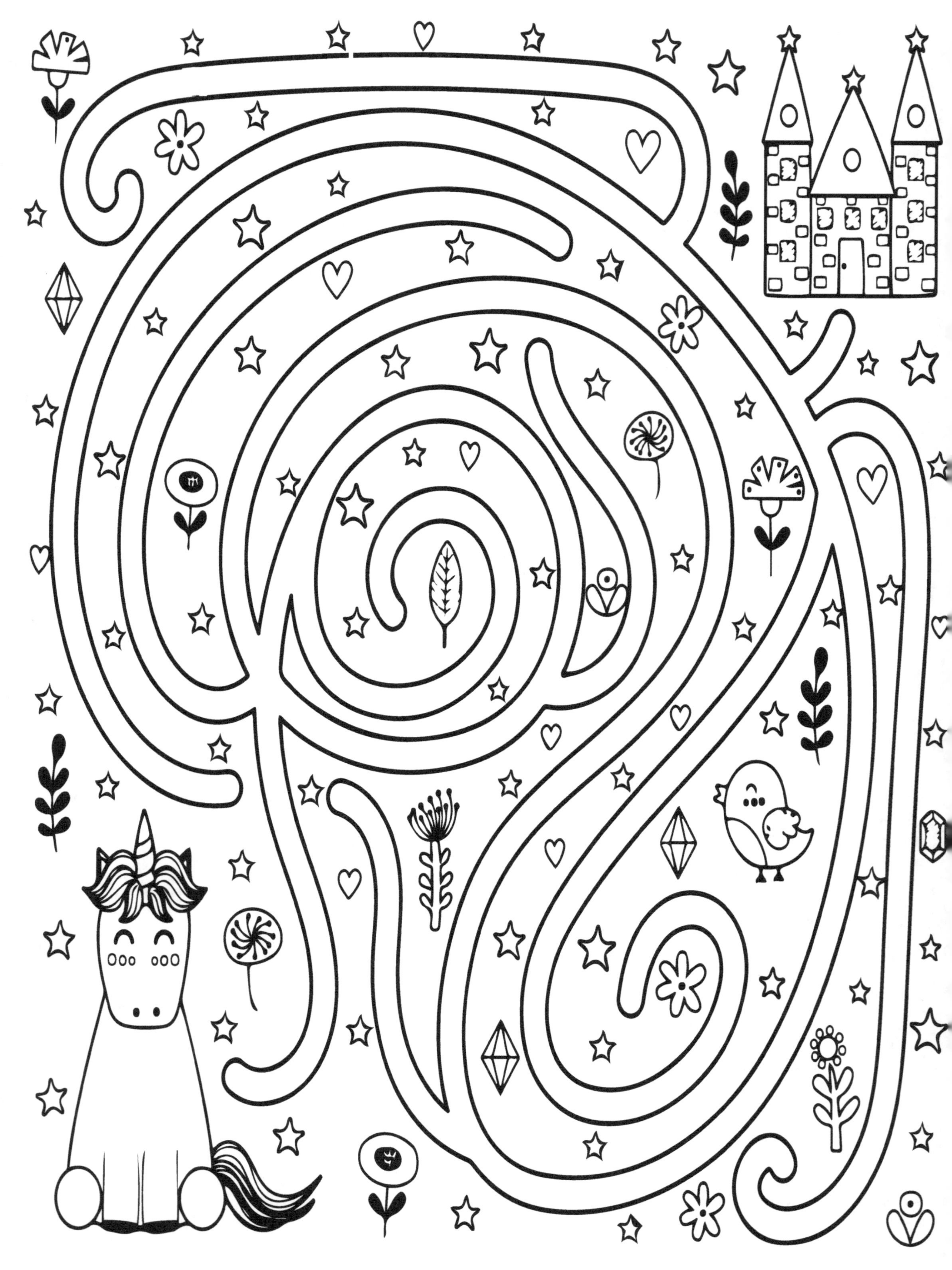

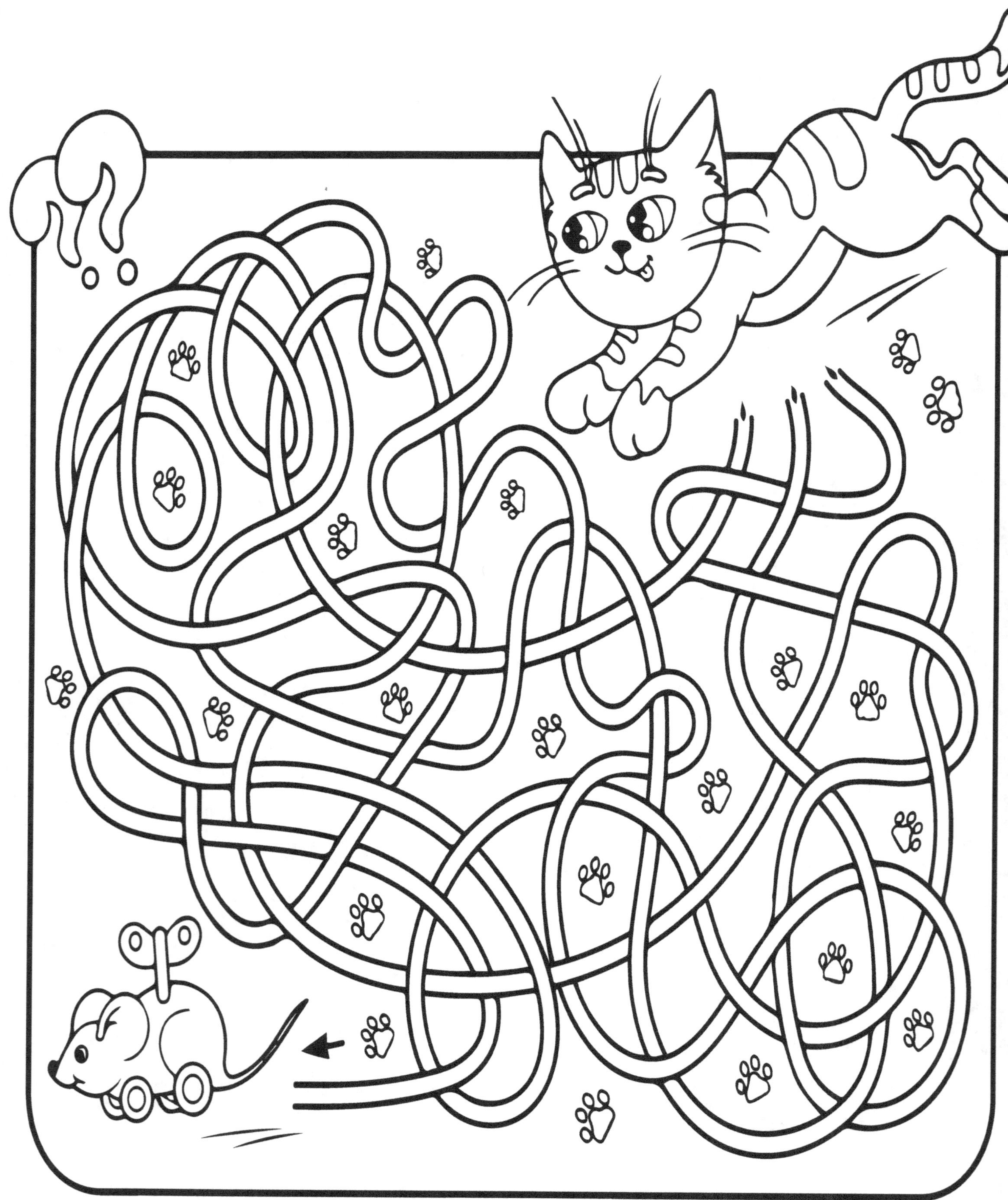

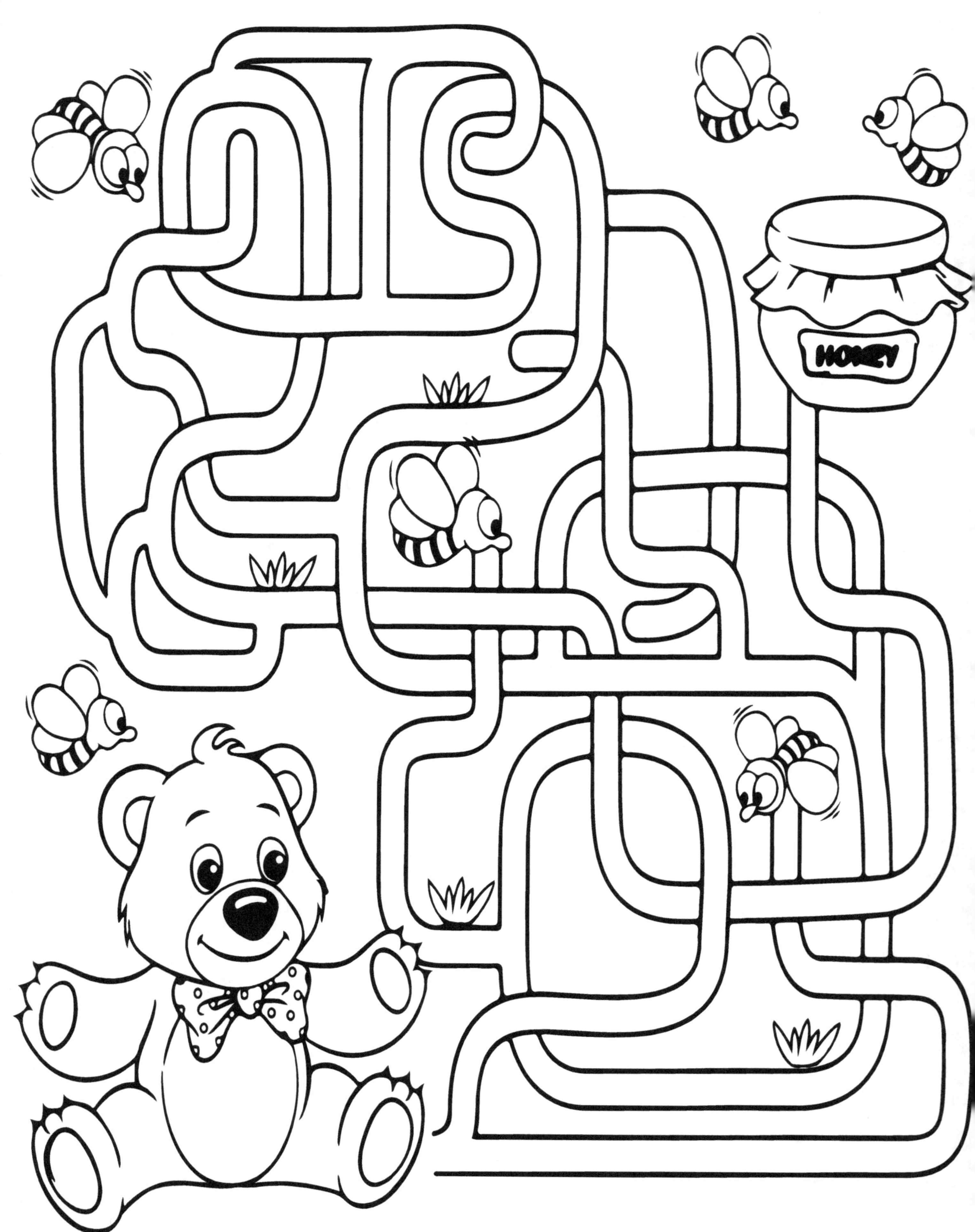

HONEY

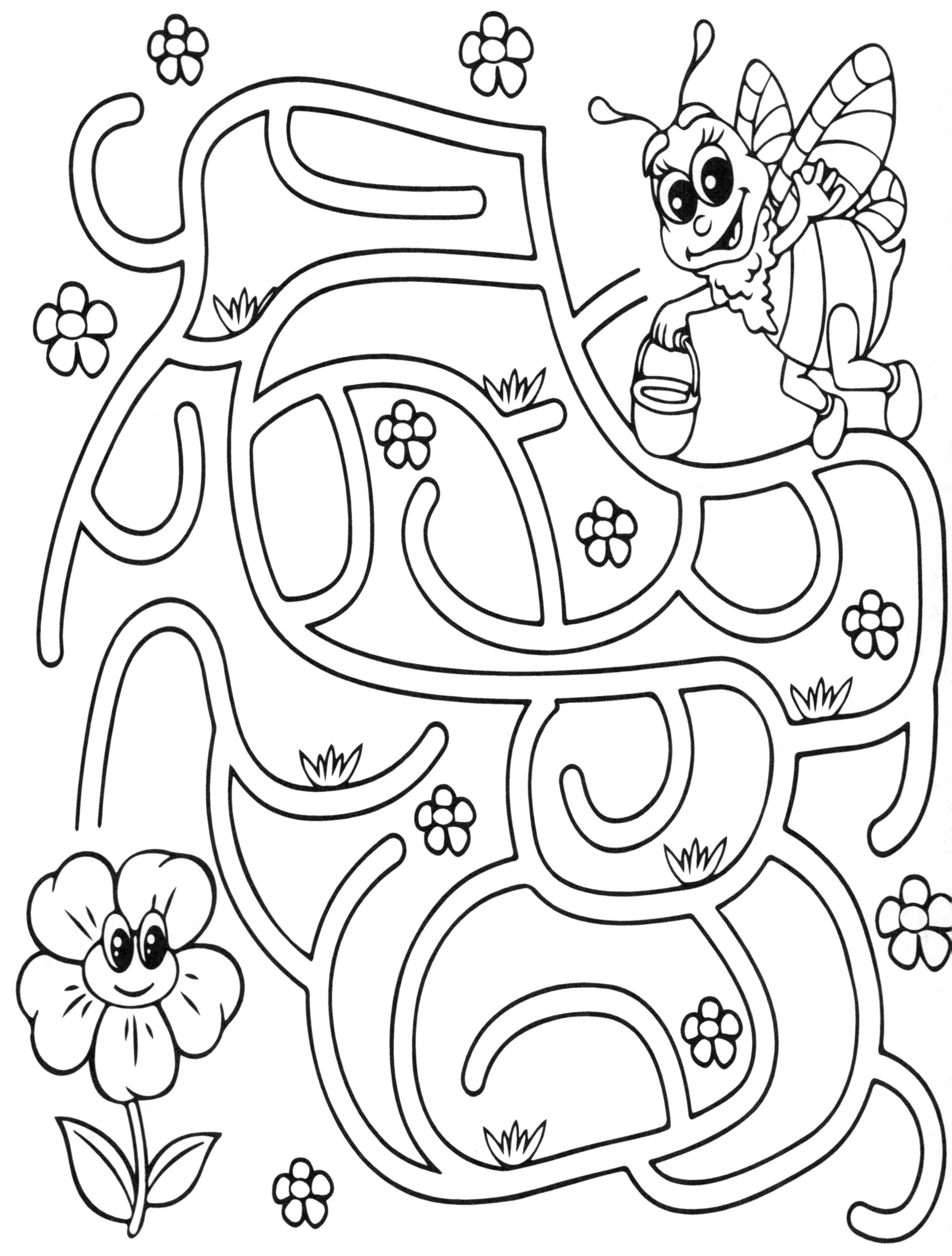

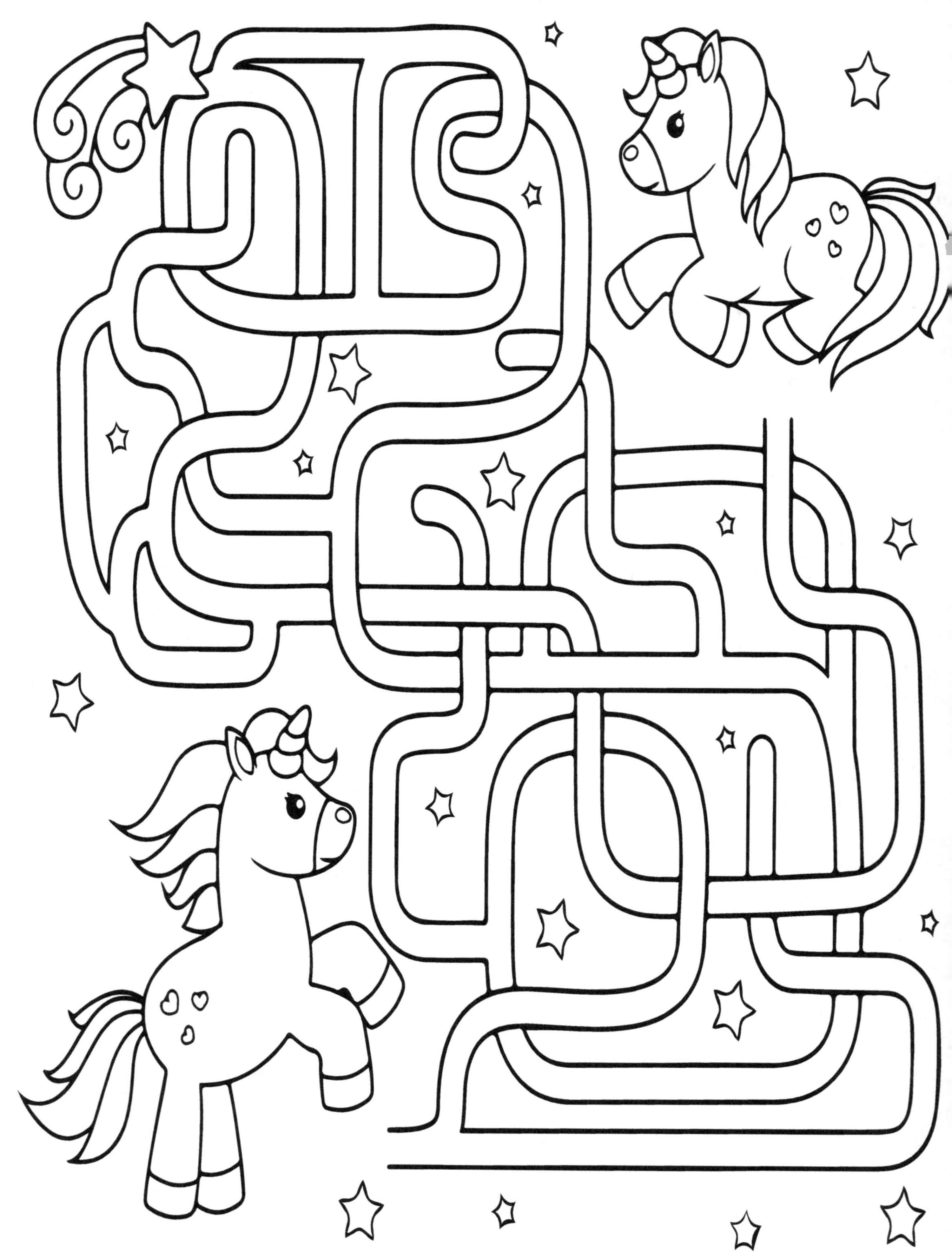

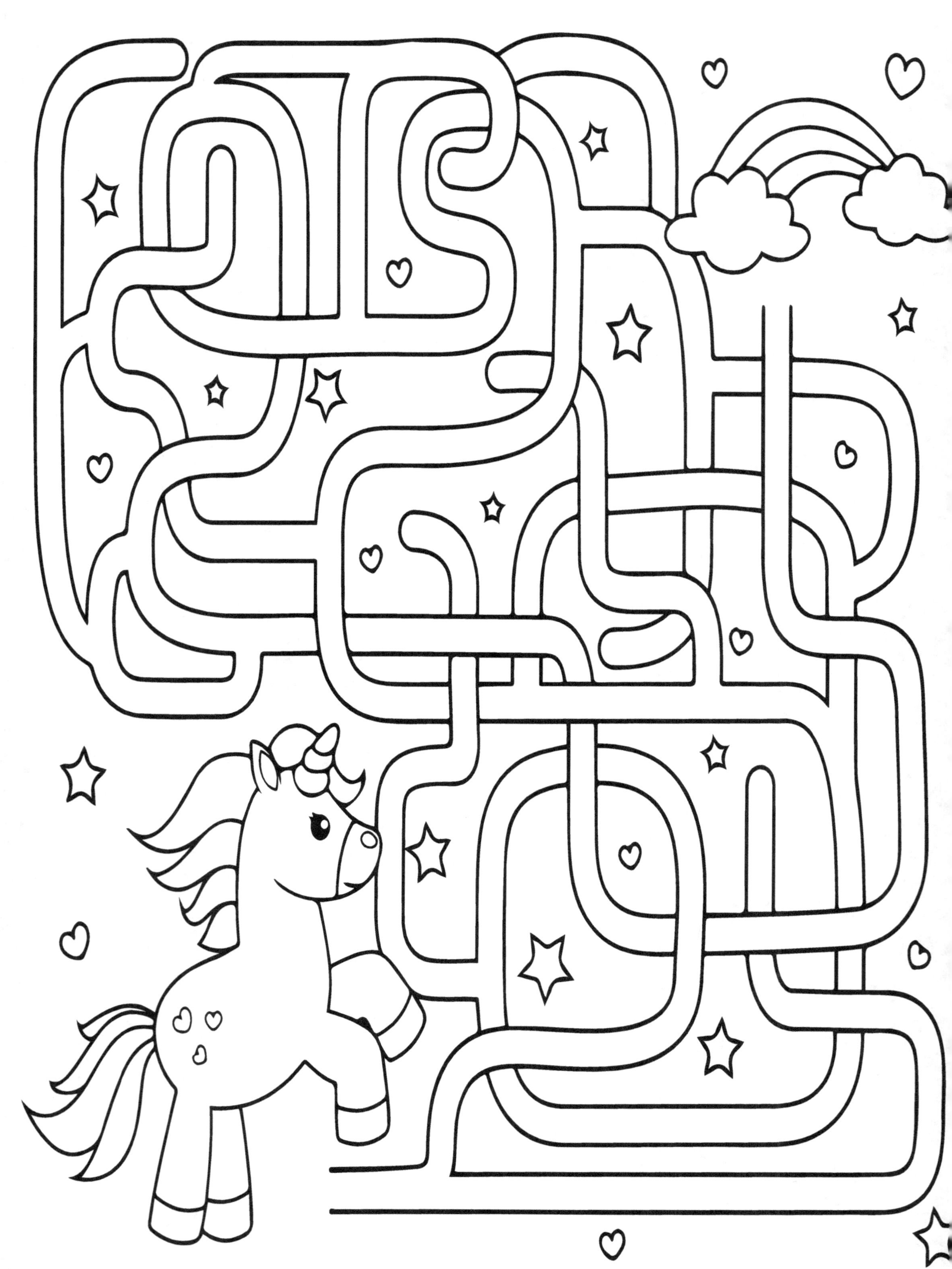

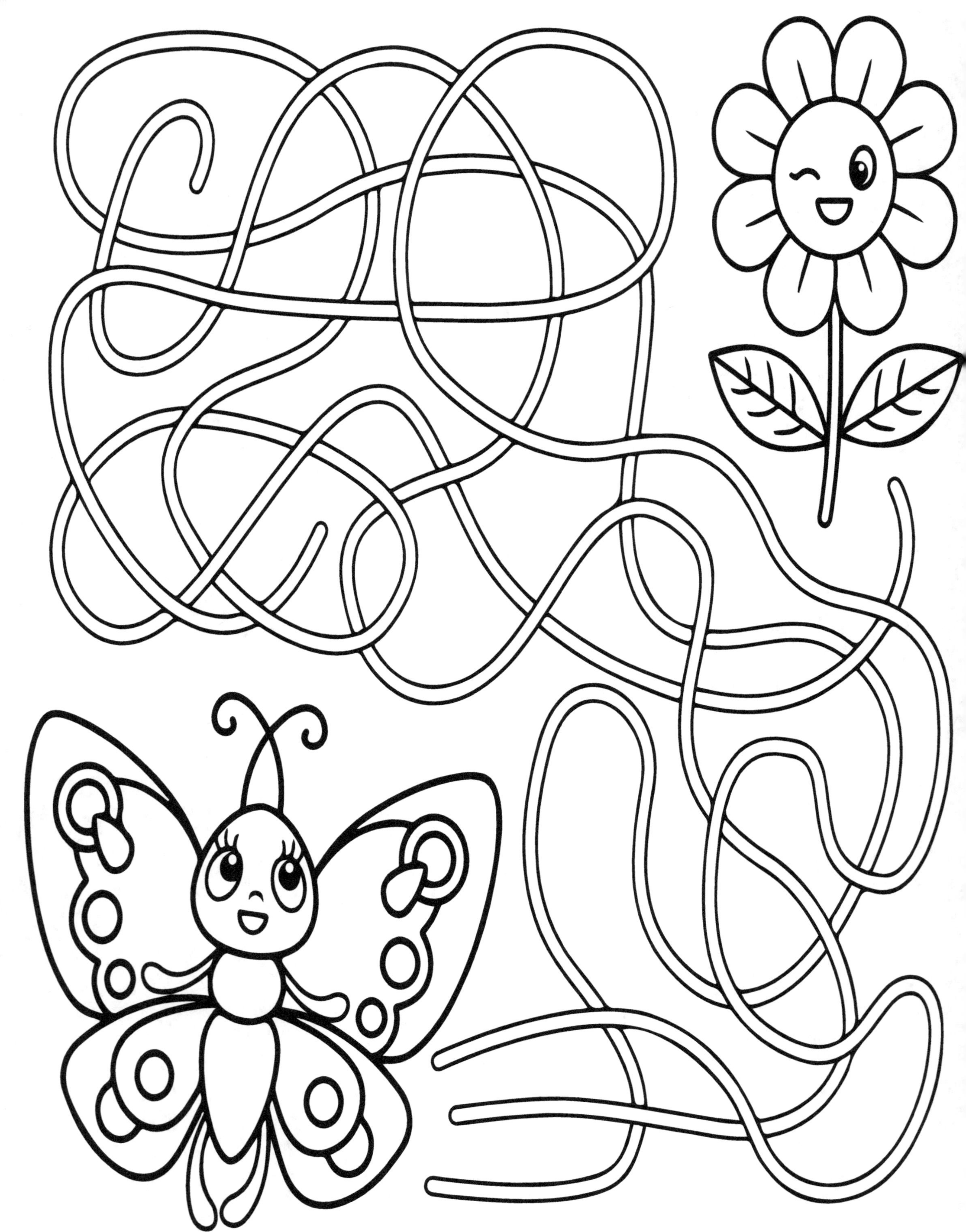

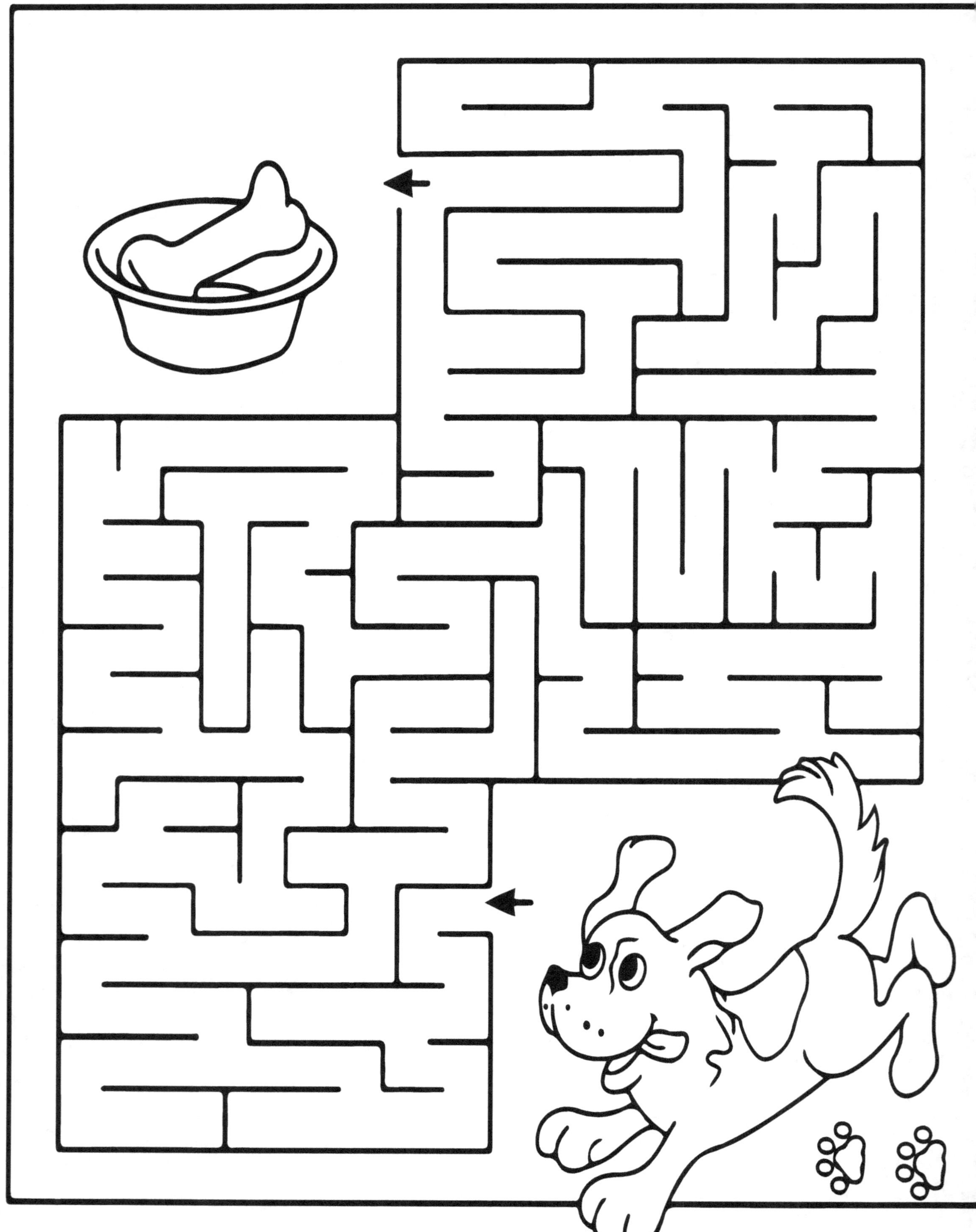

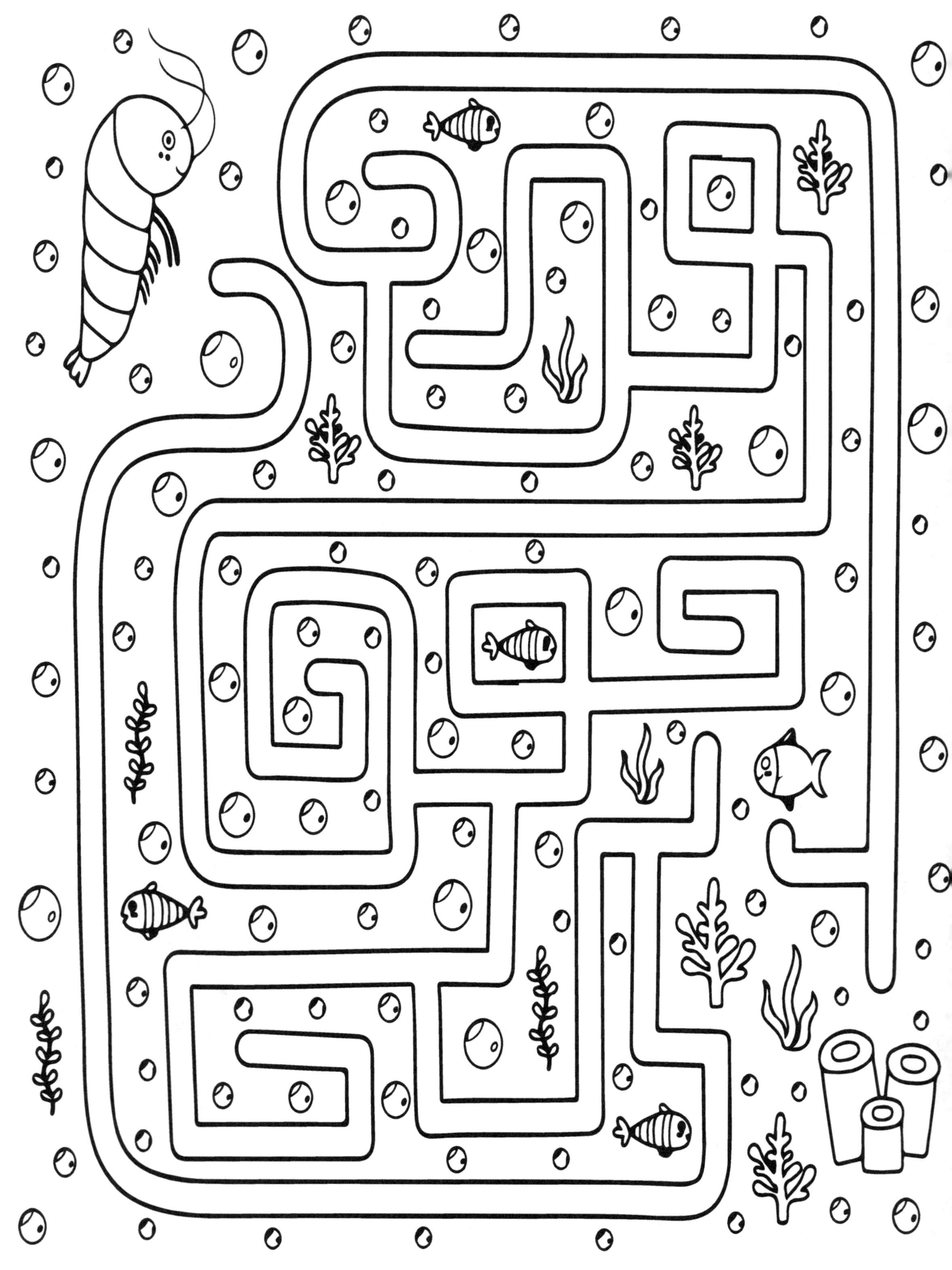

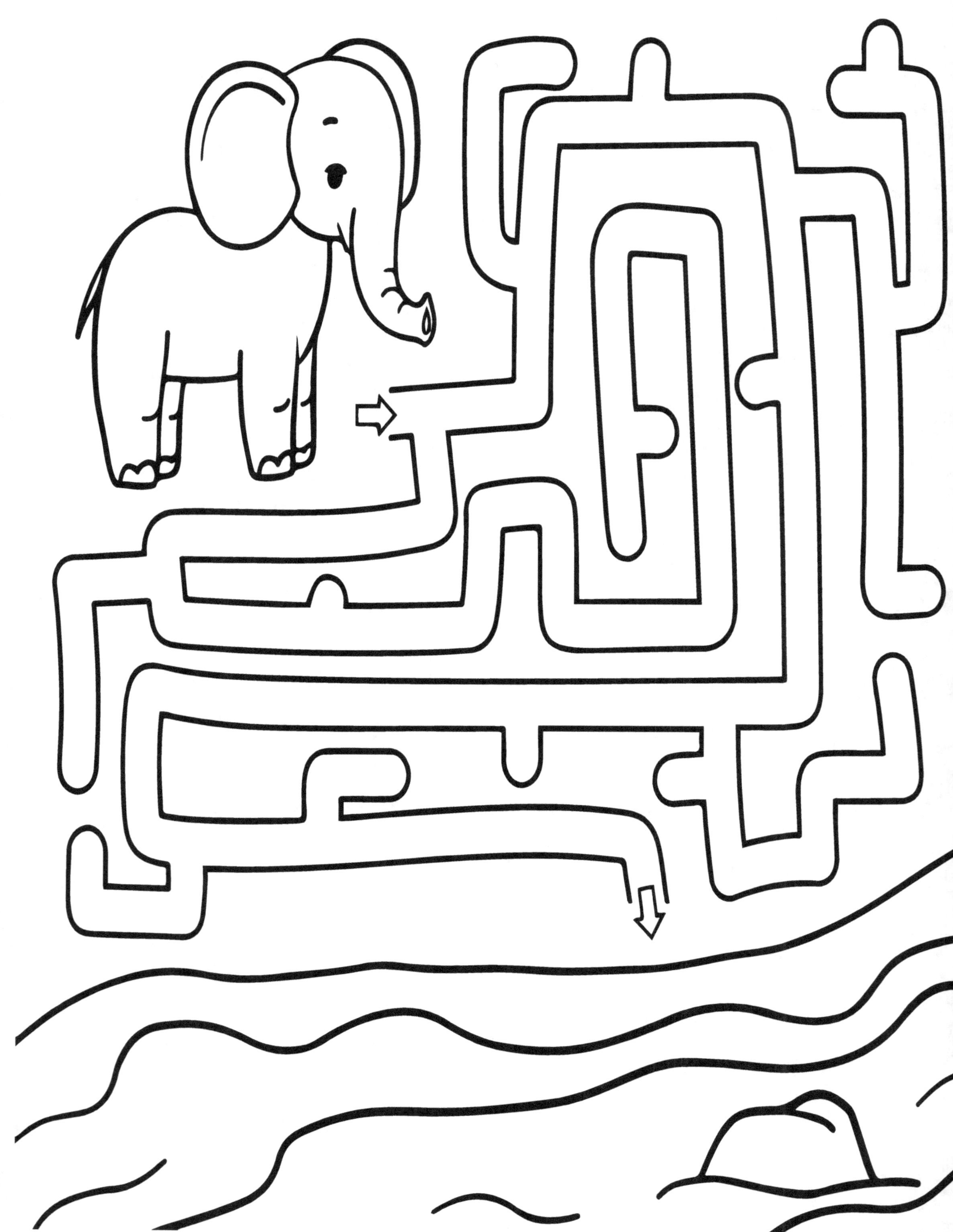

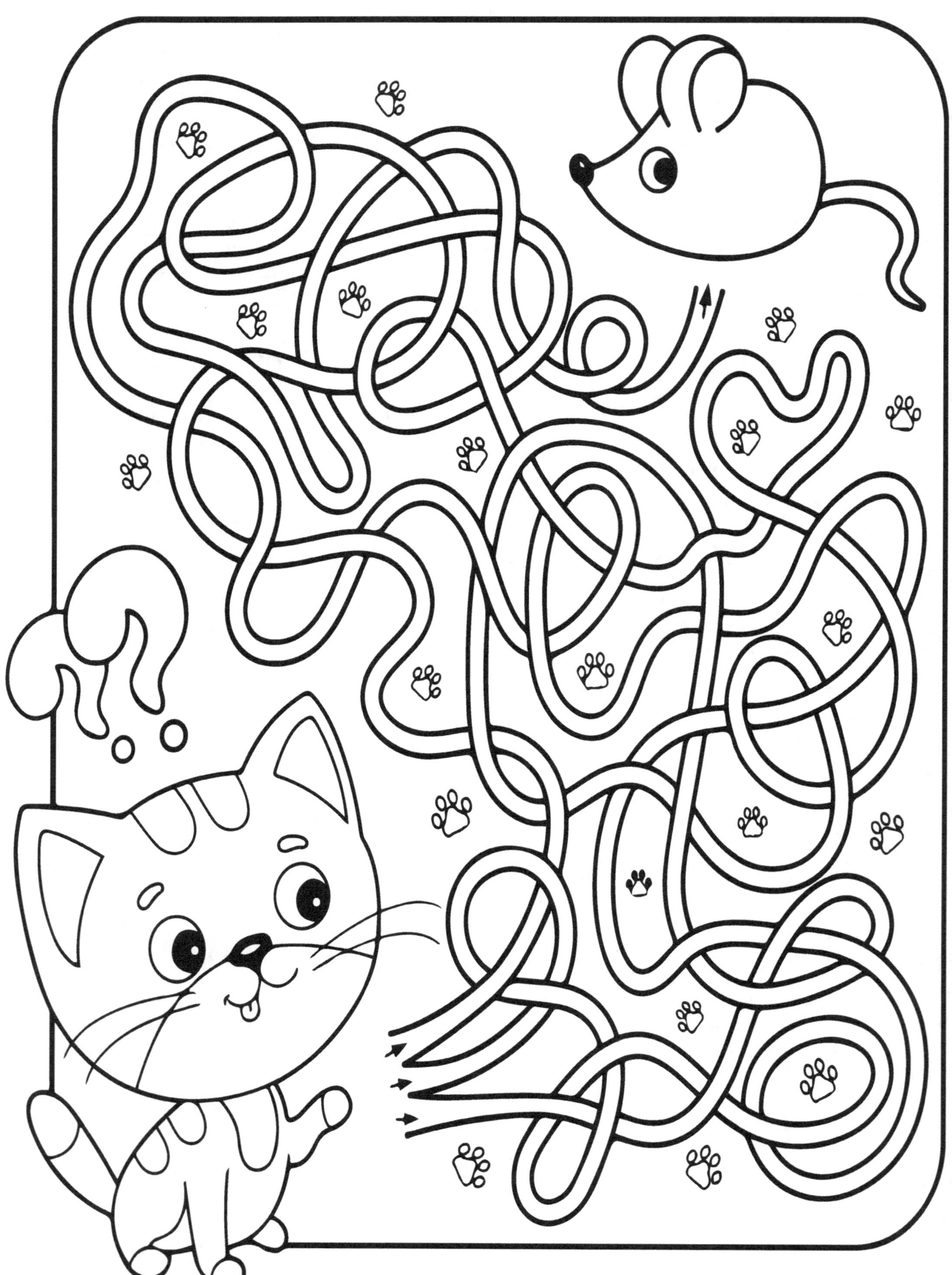

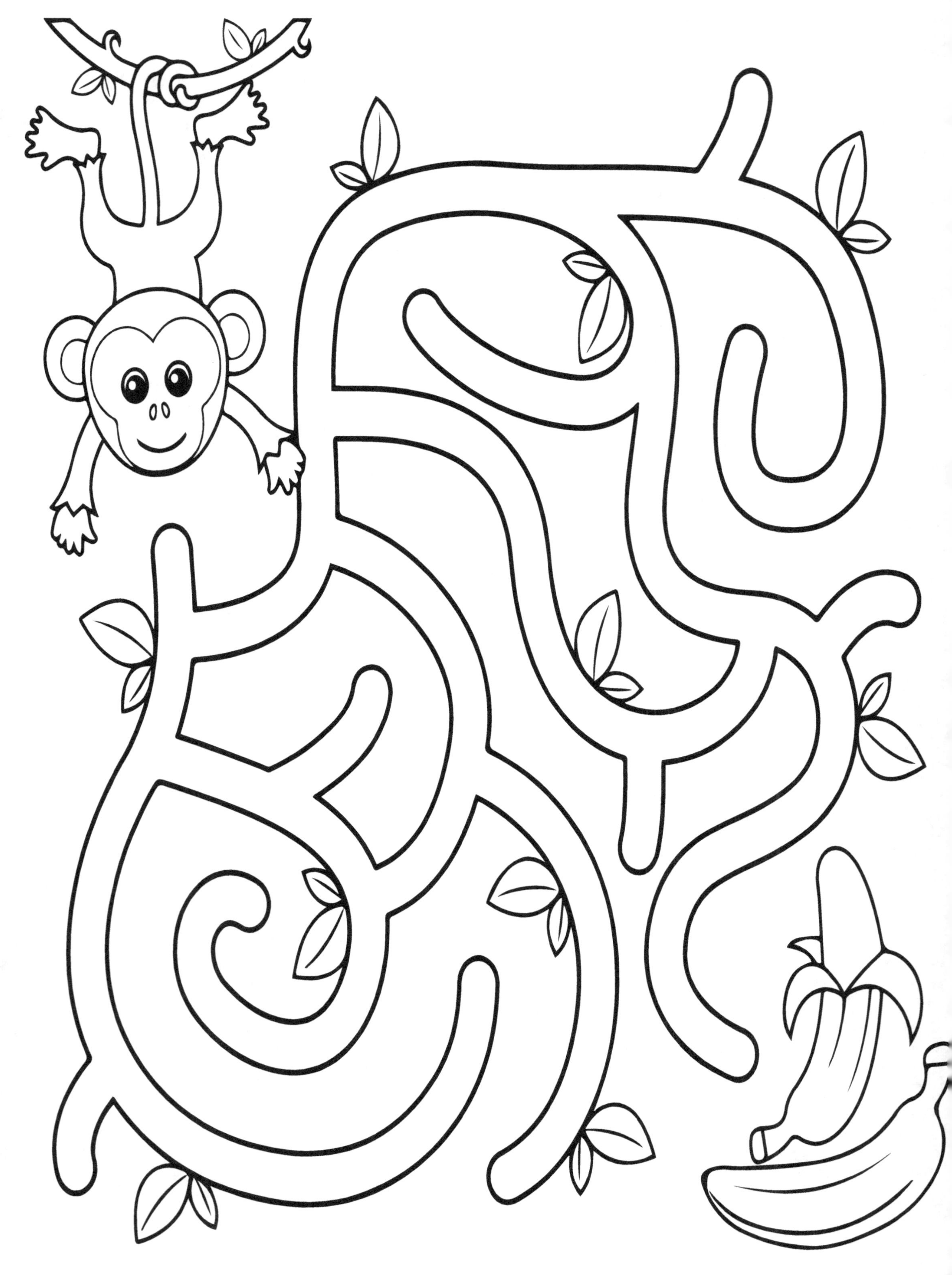

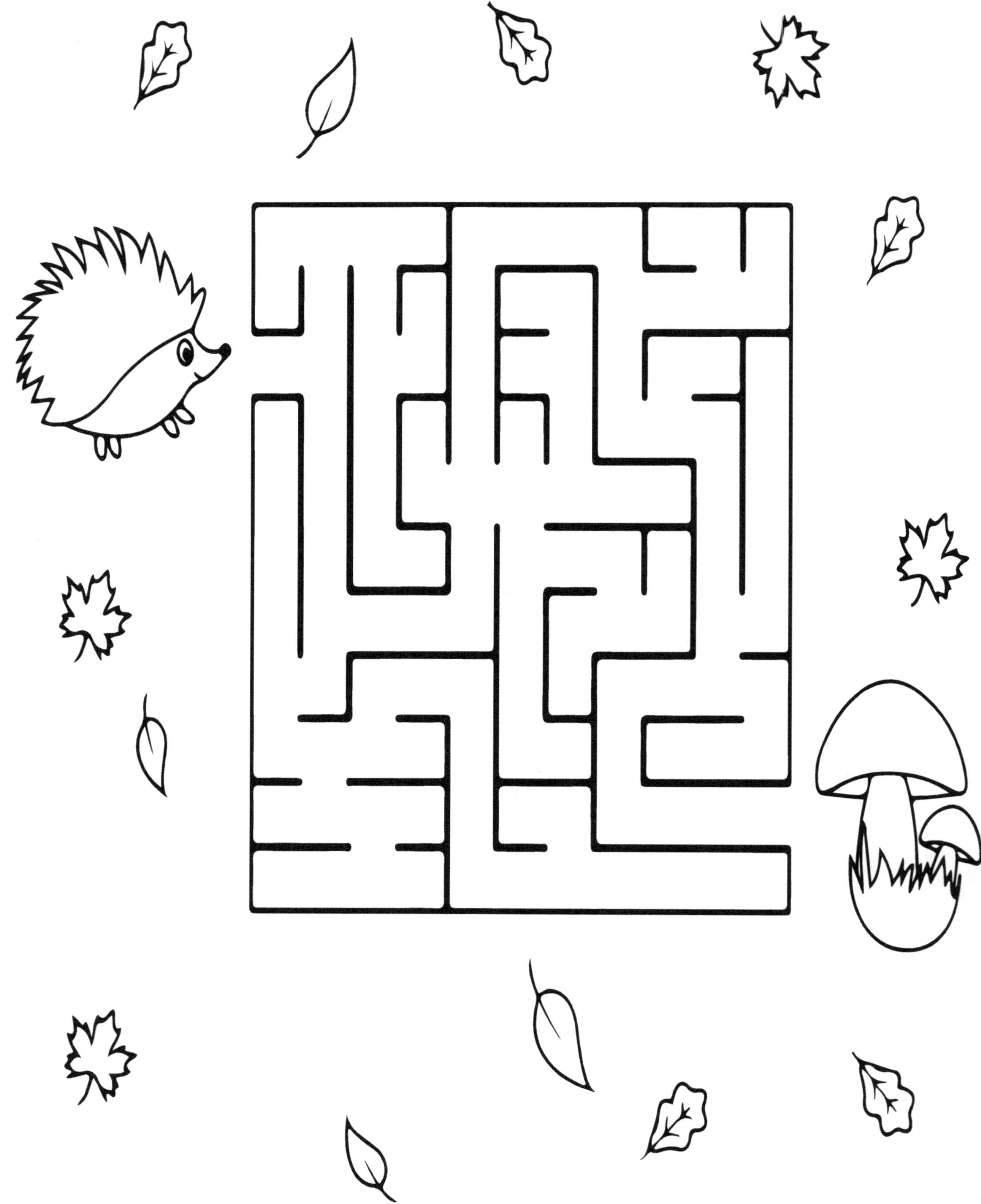

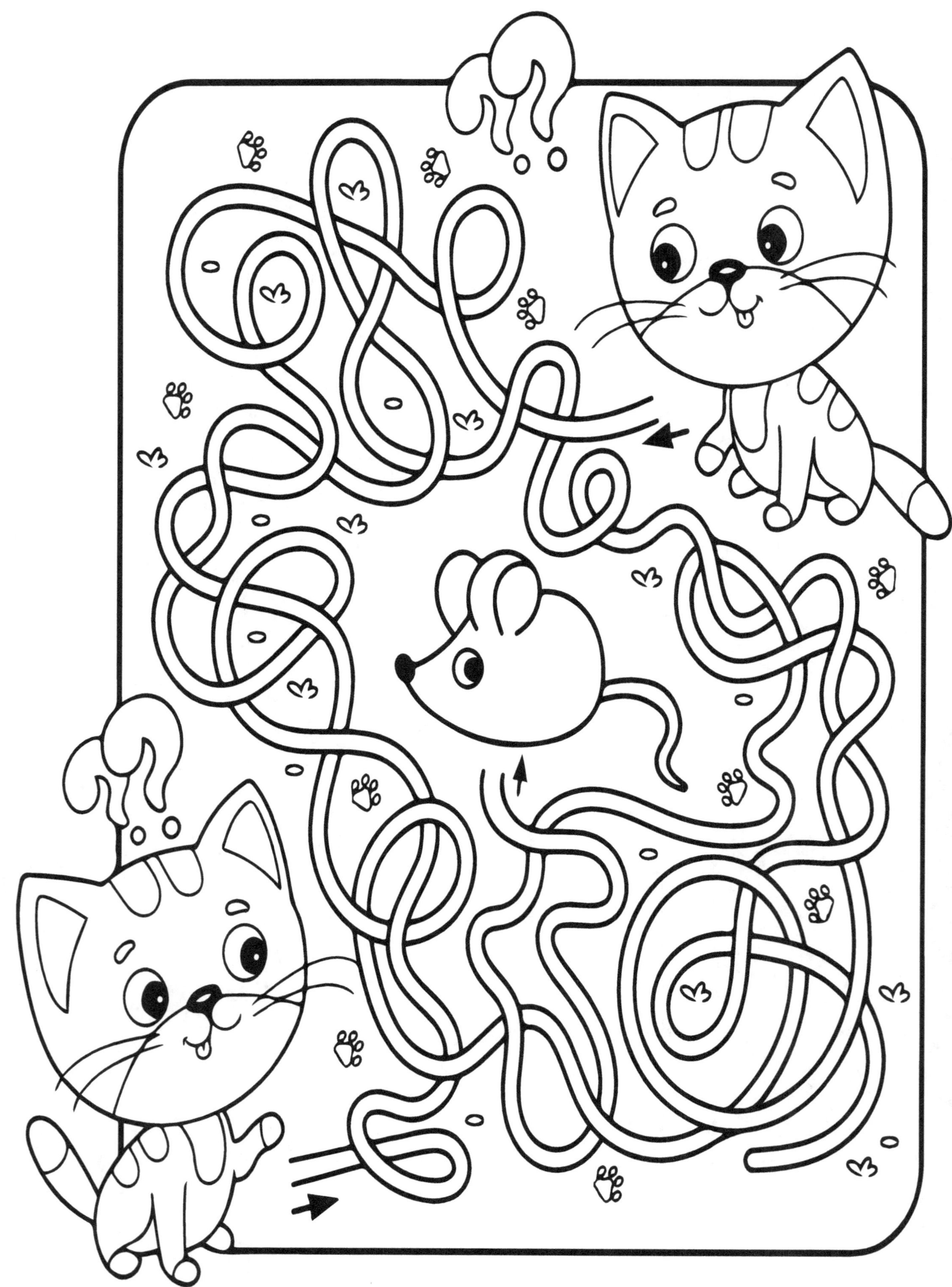

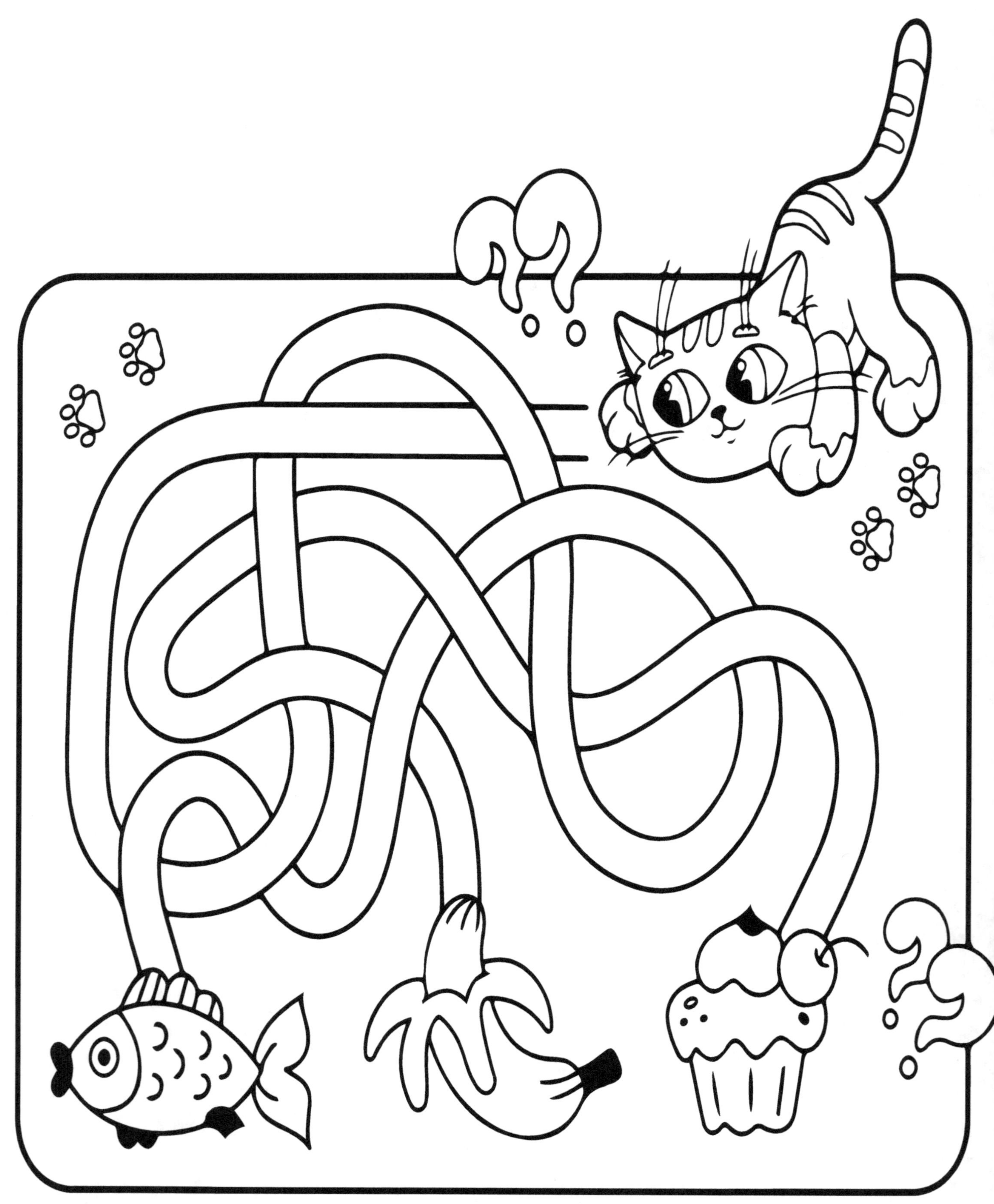

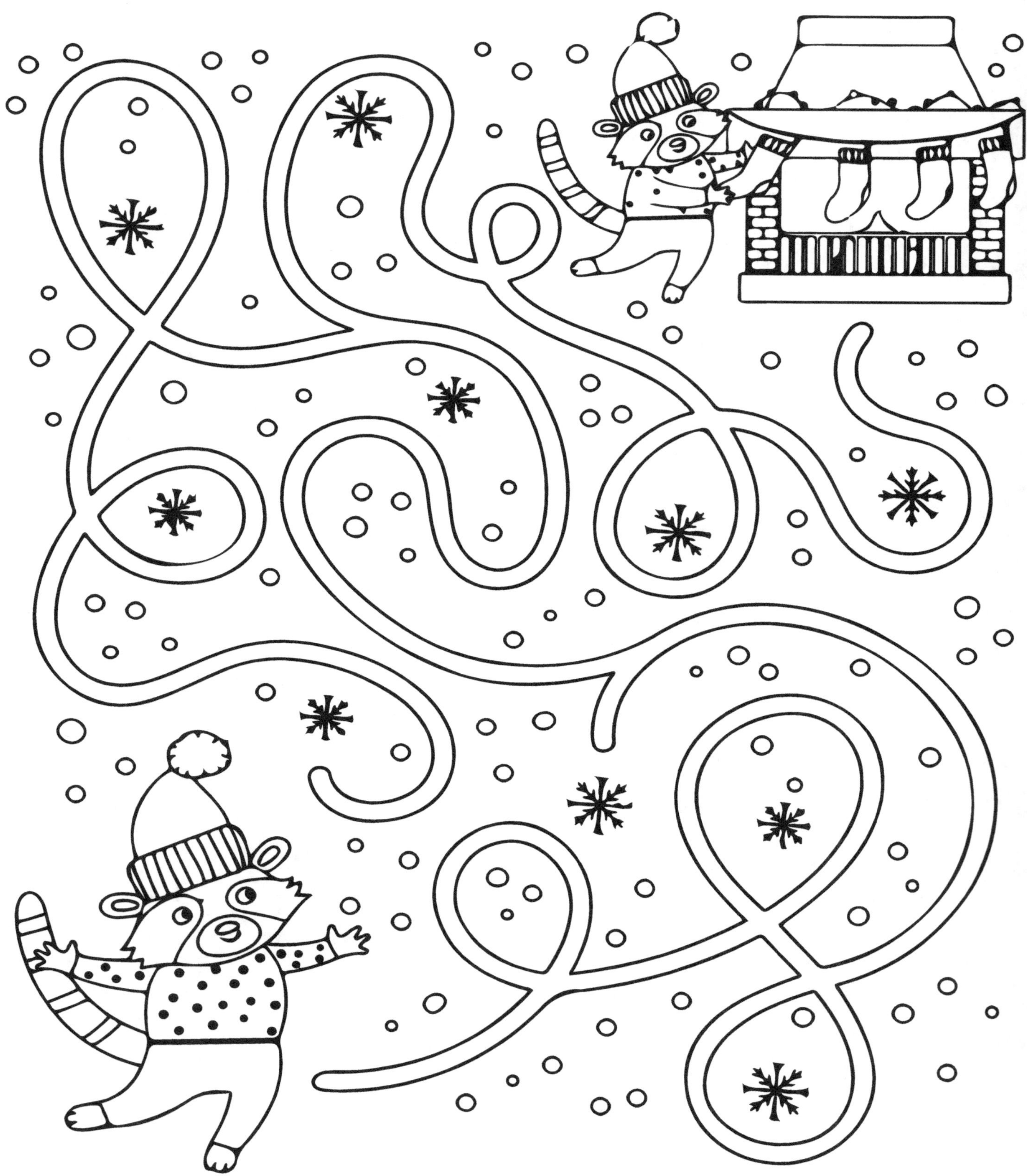

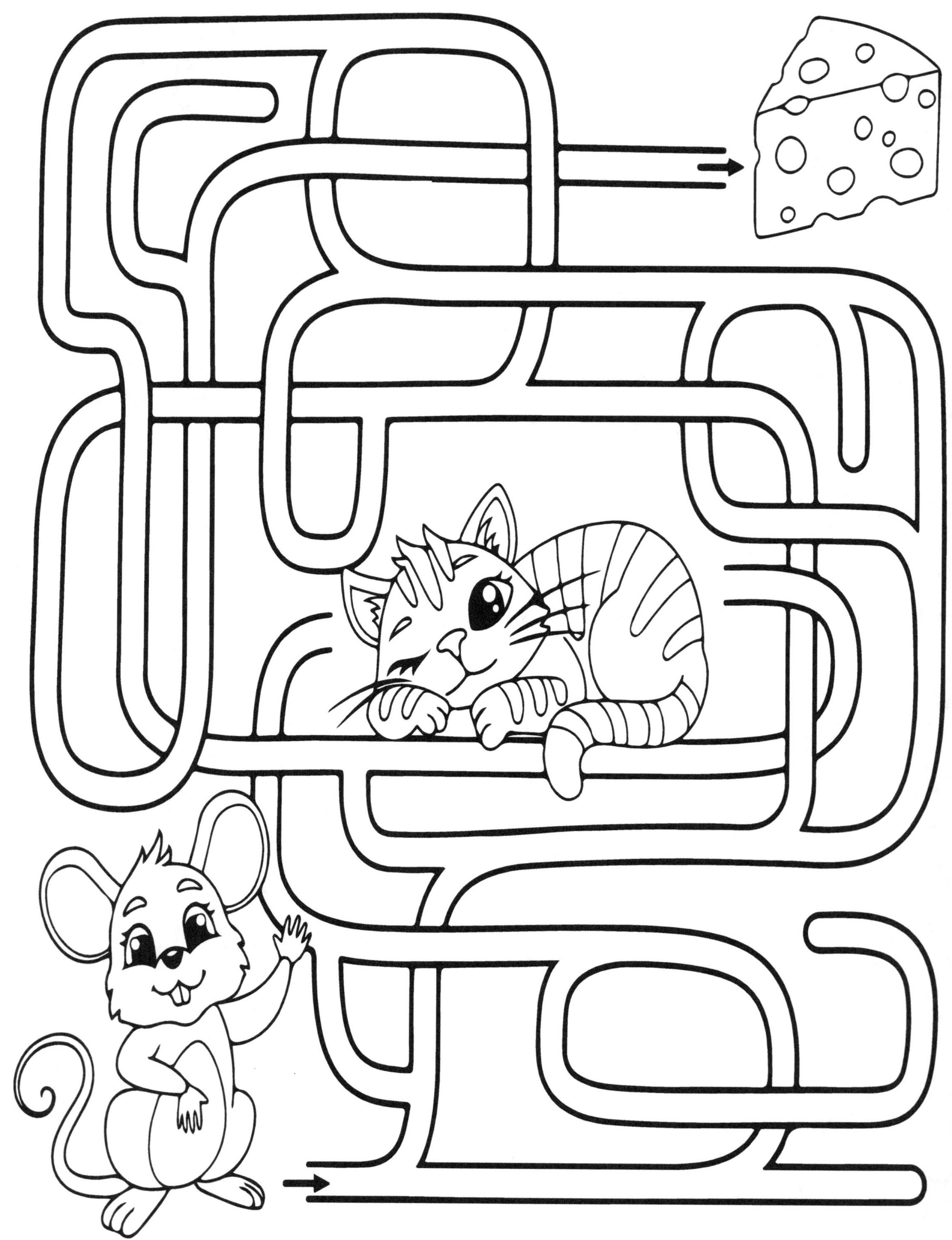

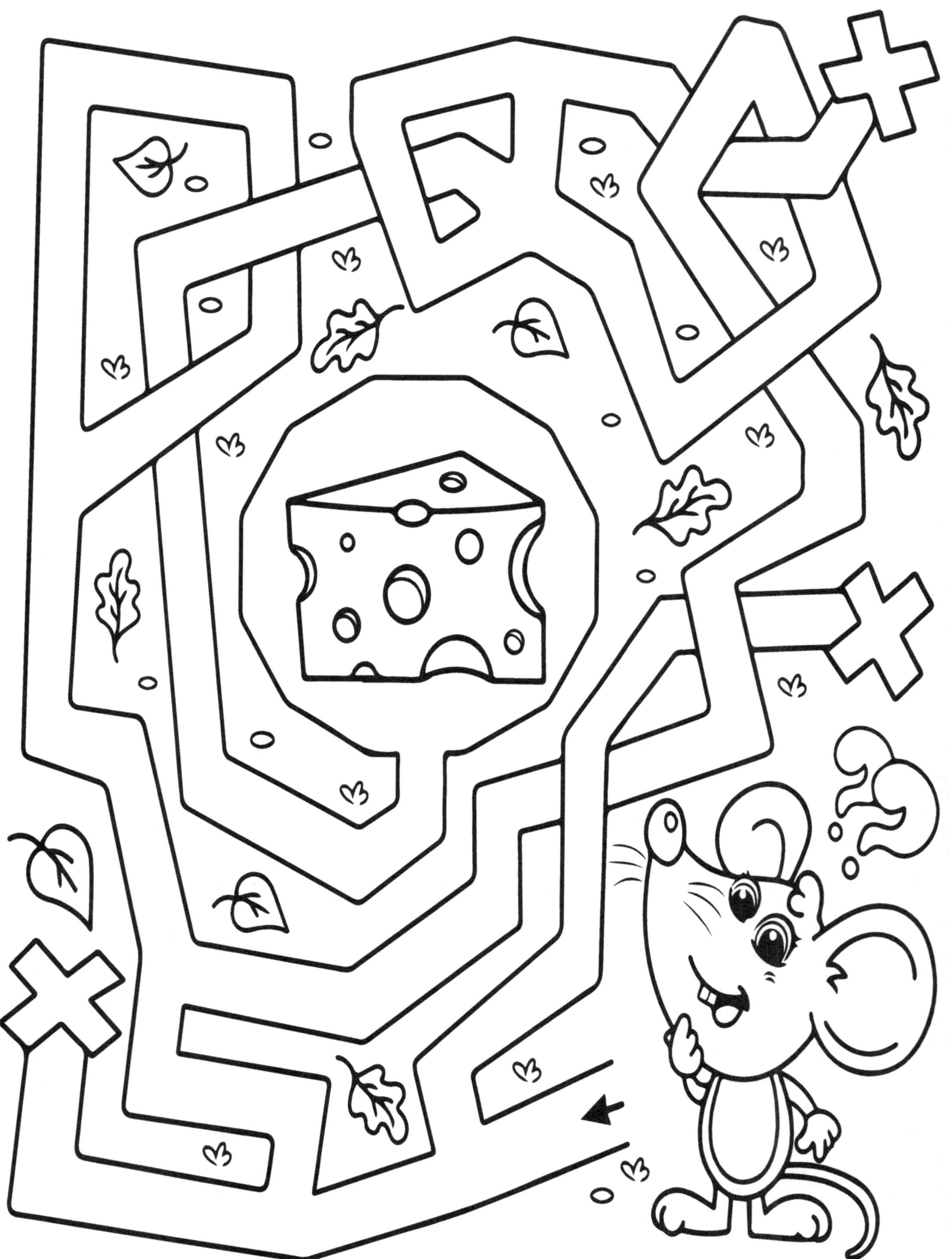

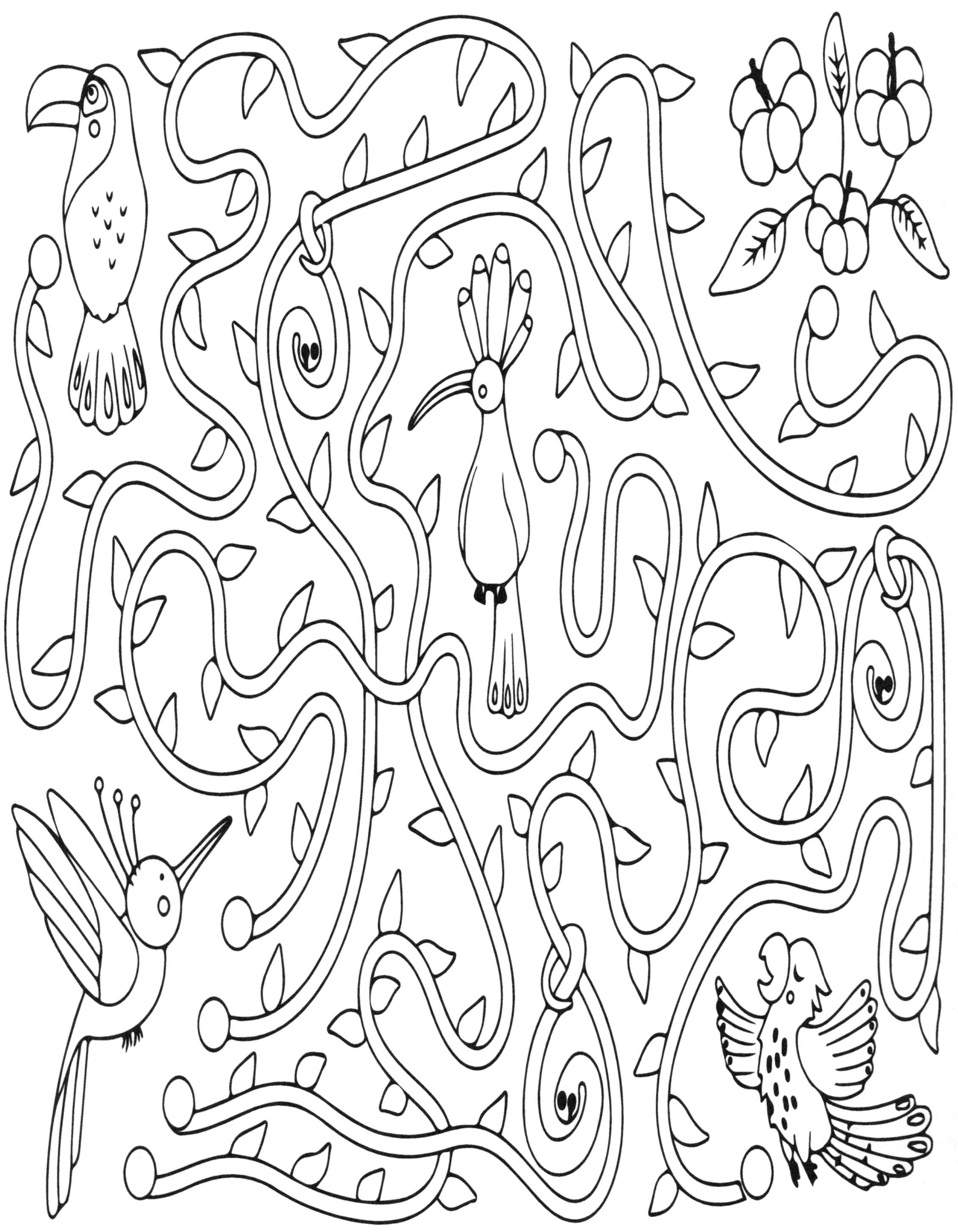

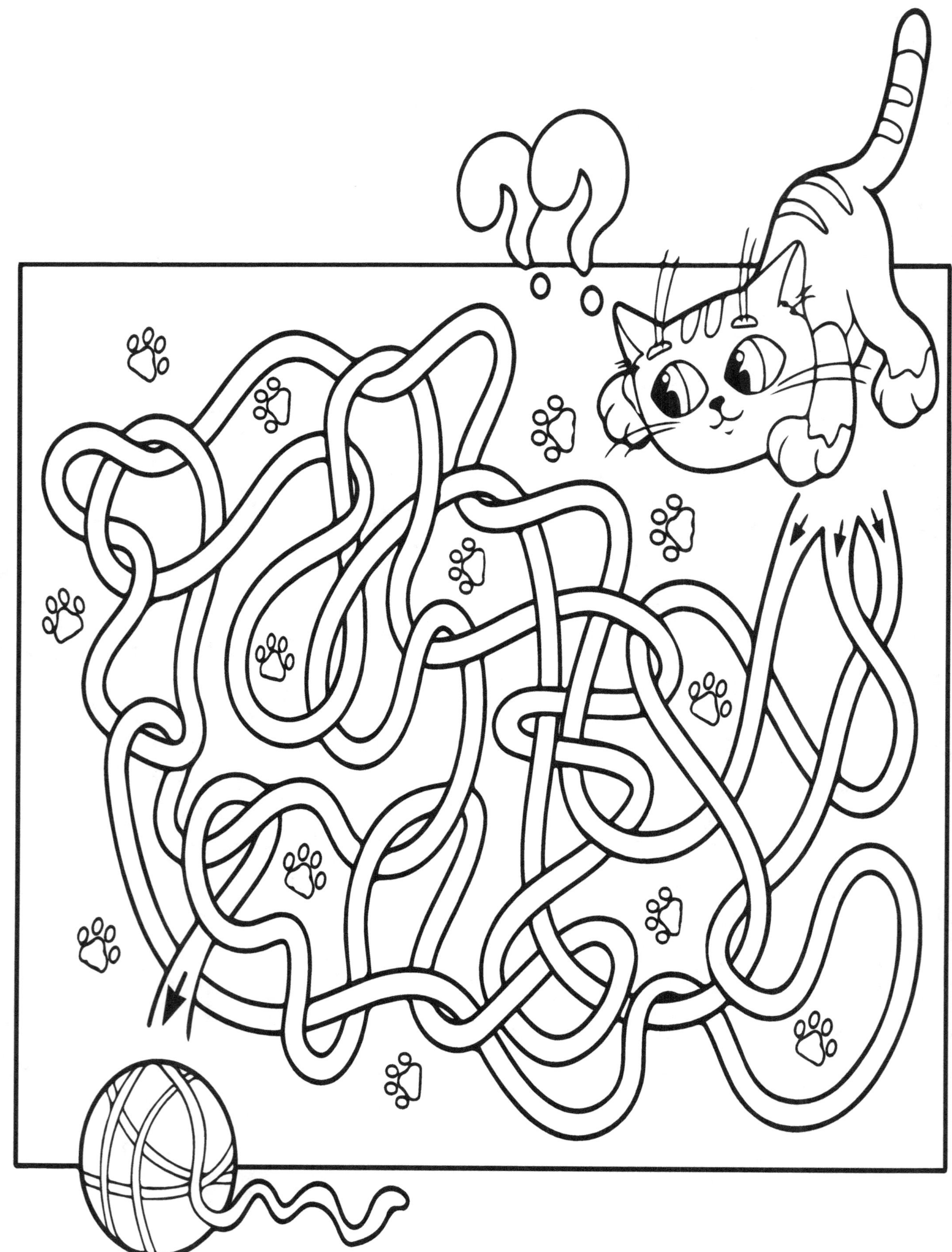

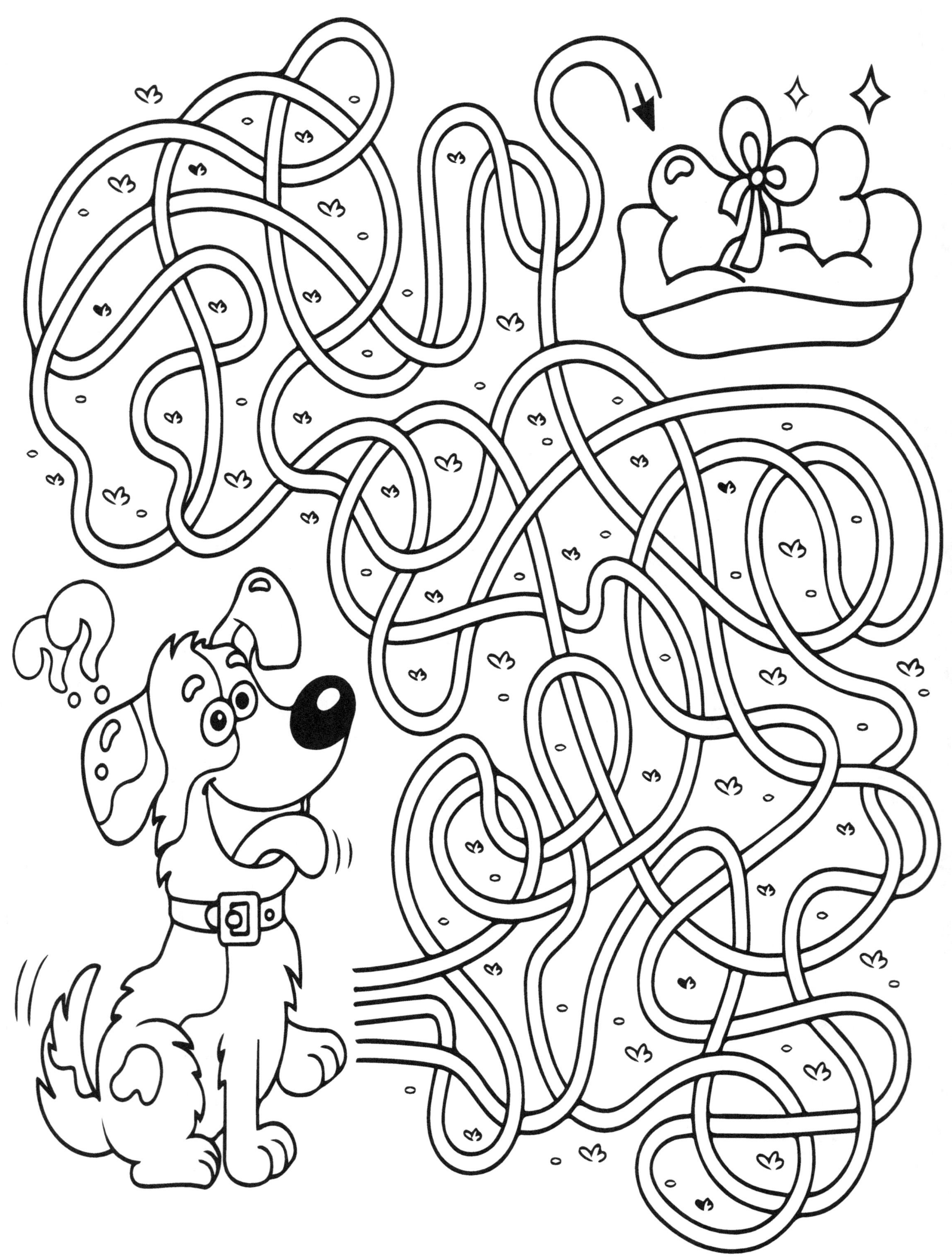

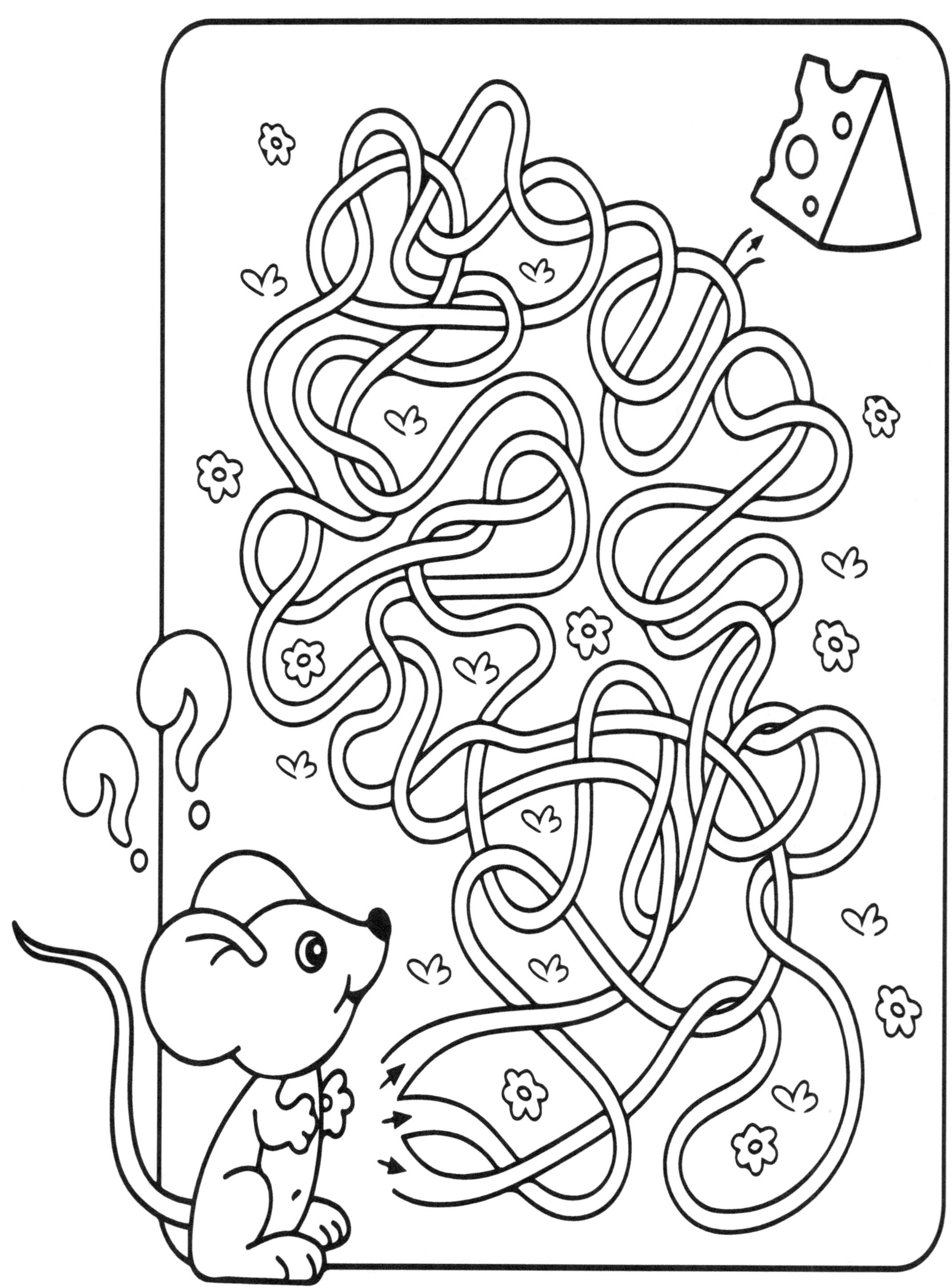

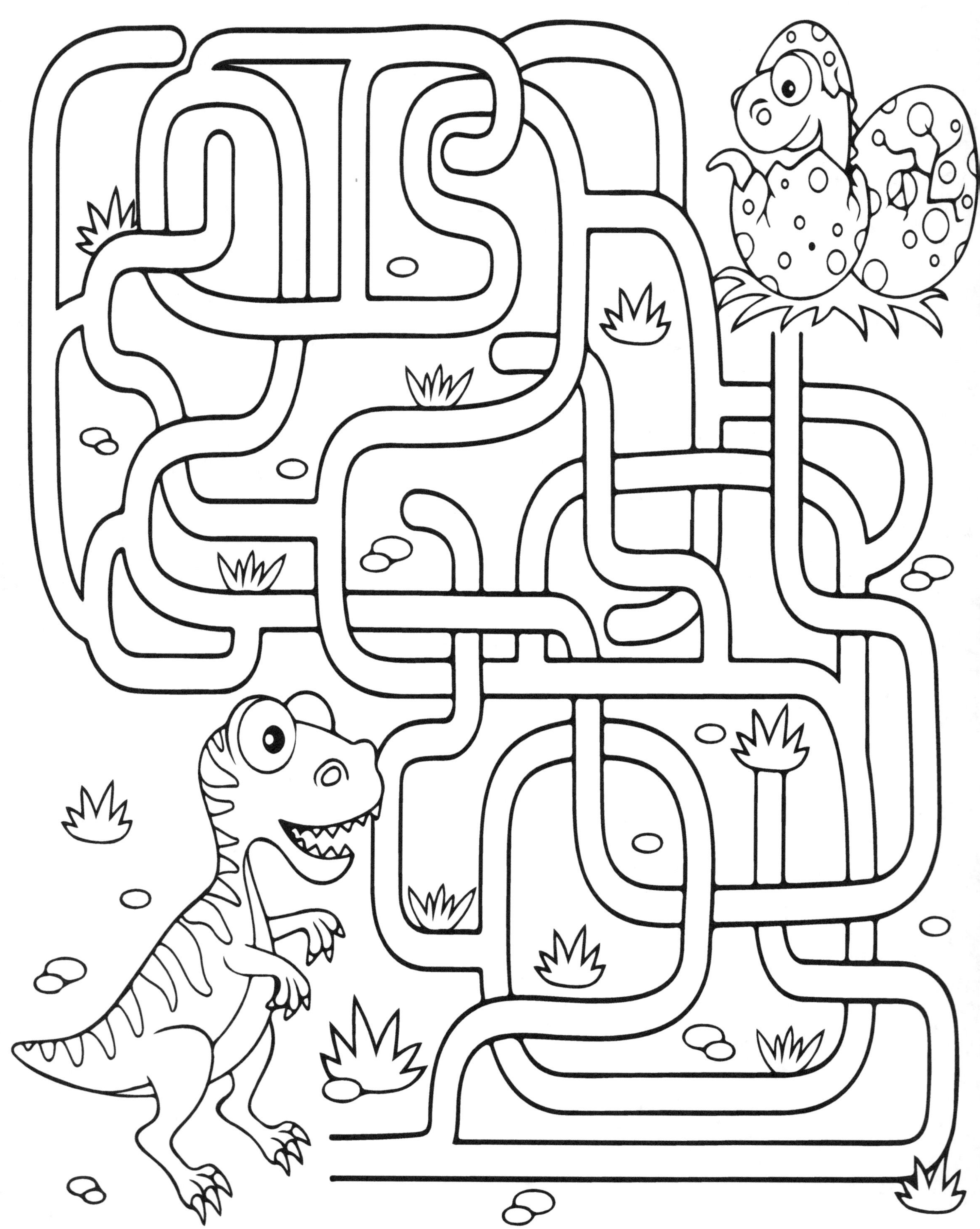

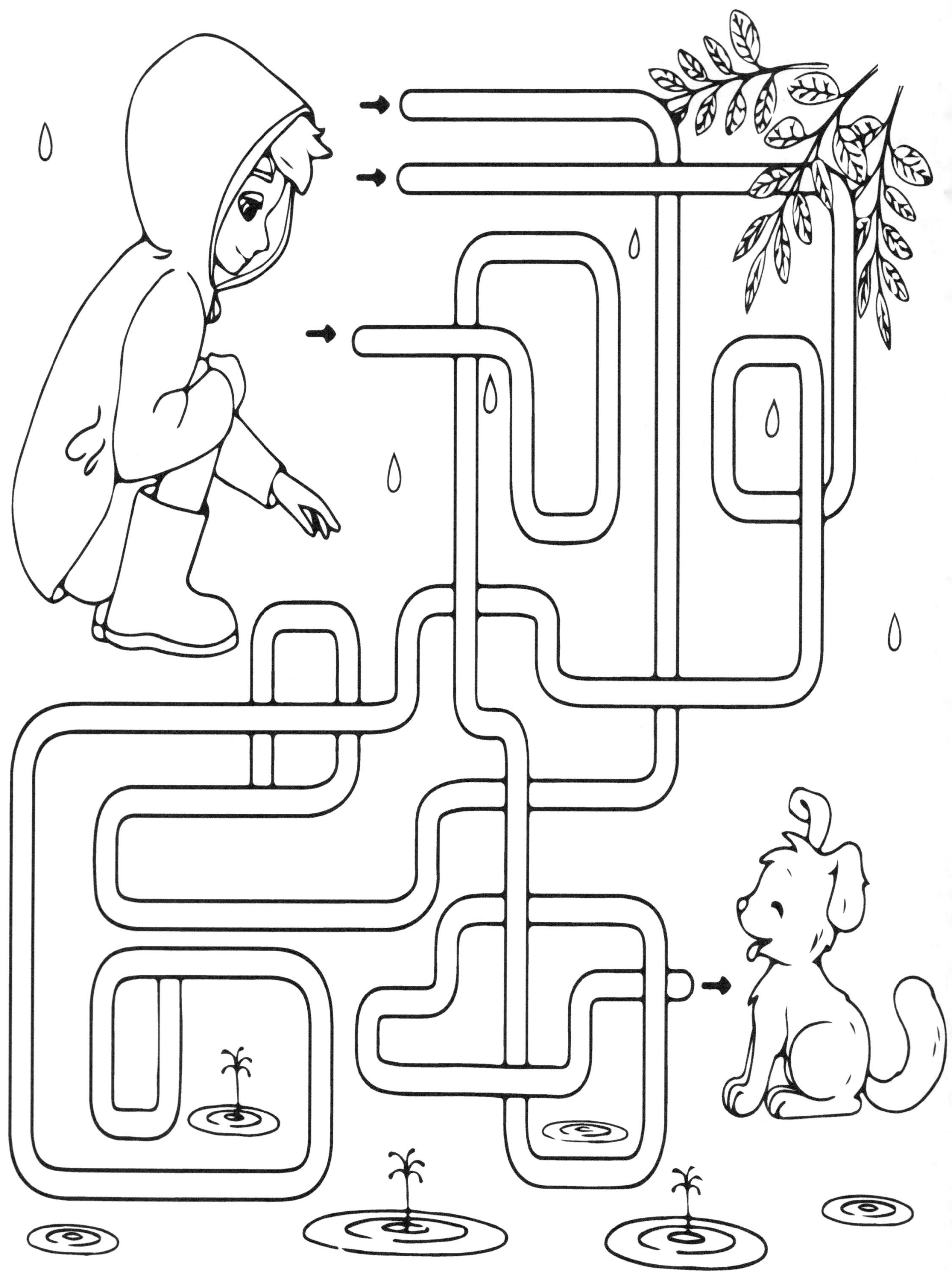

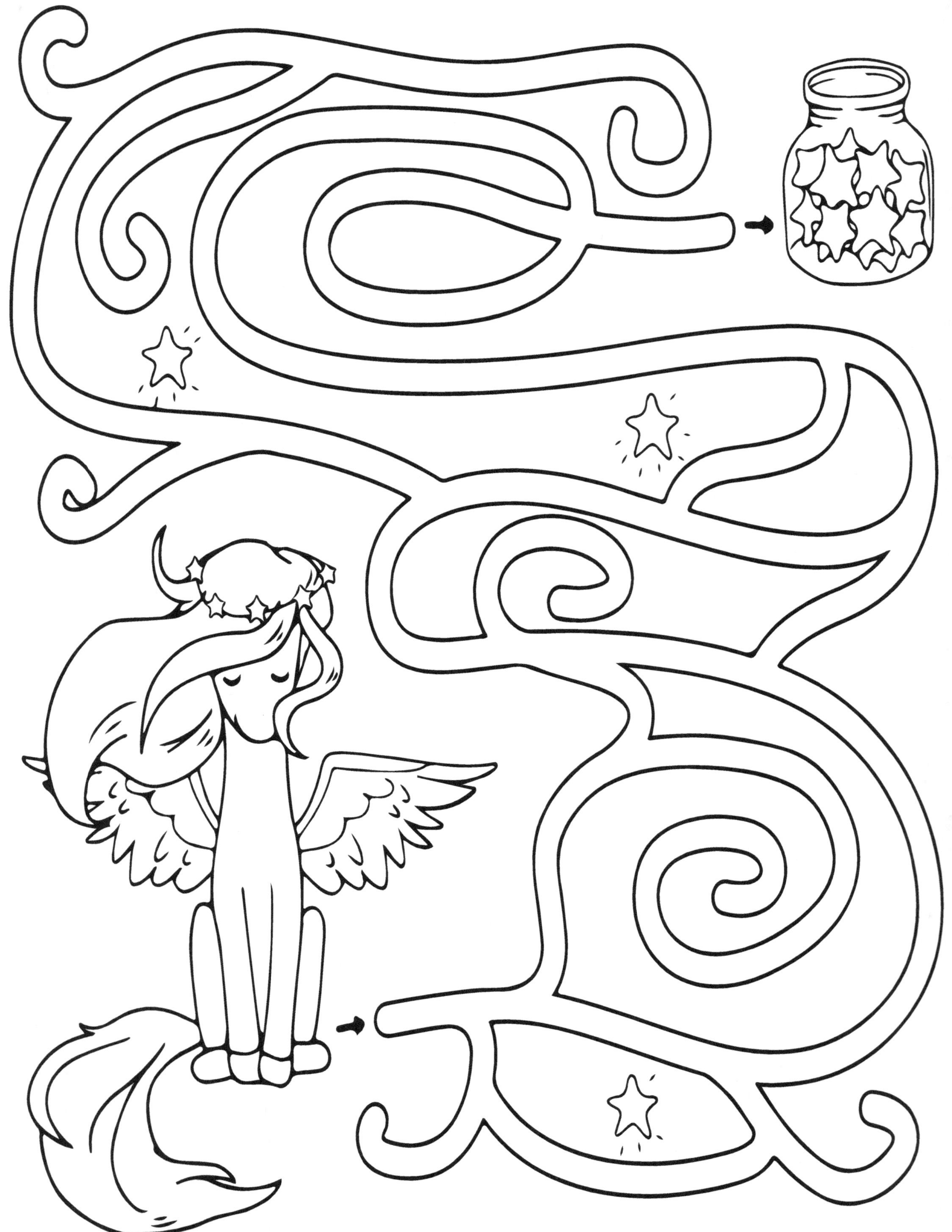

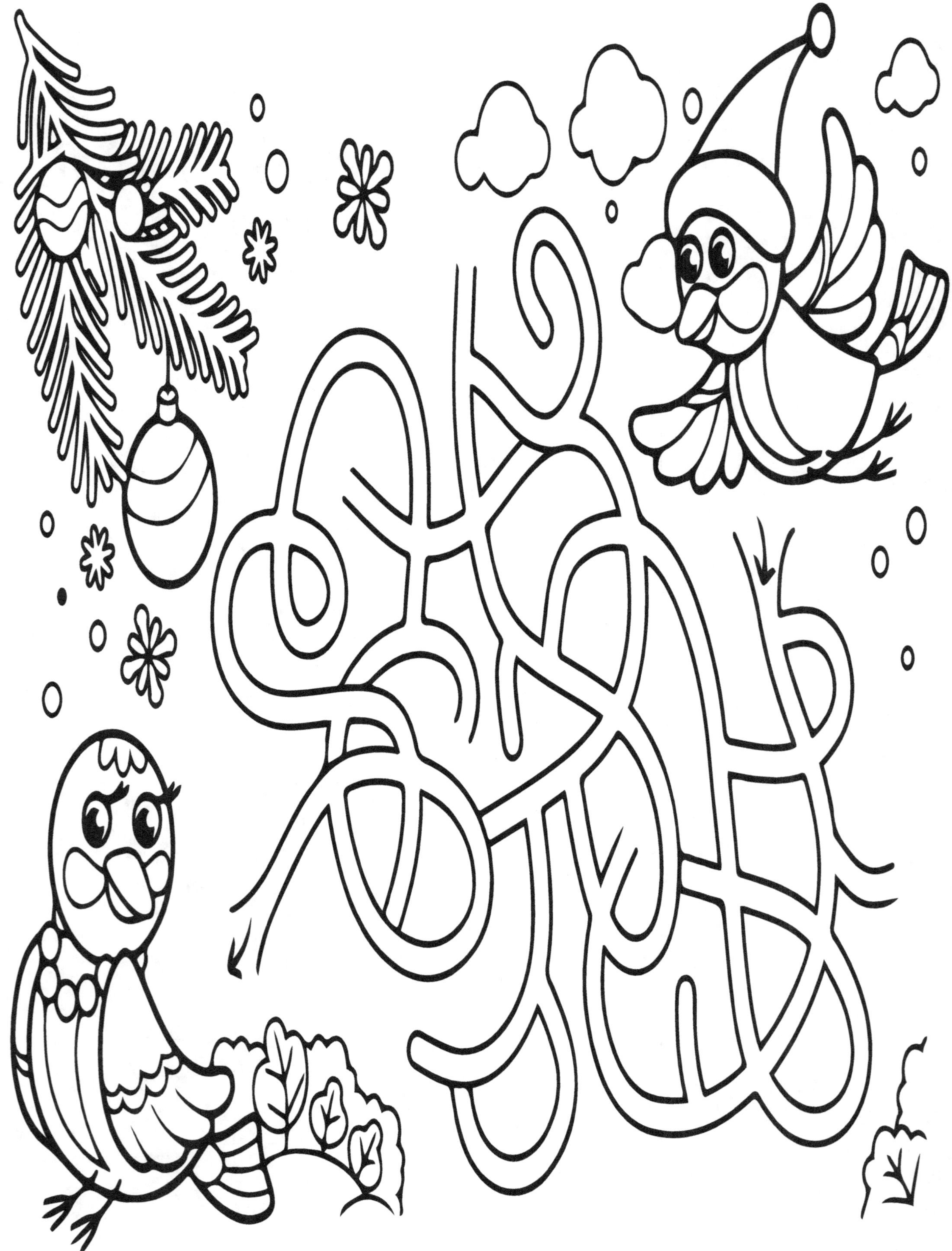

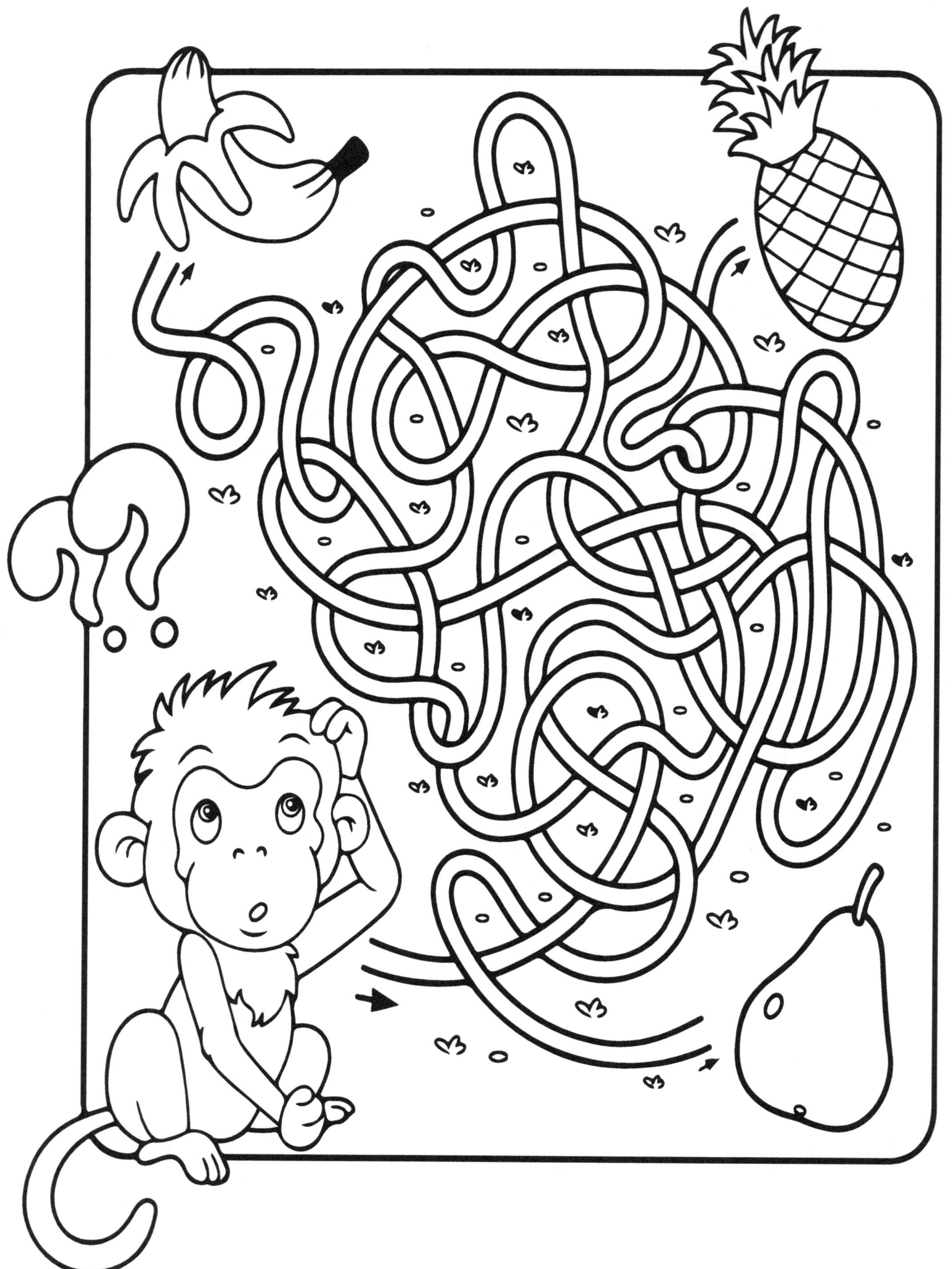

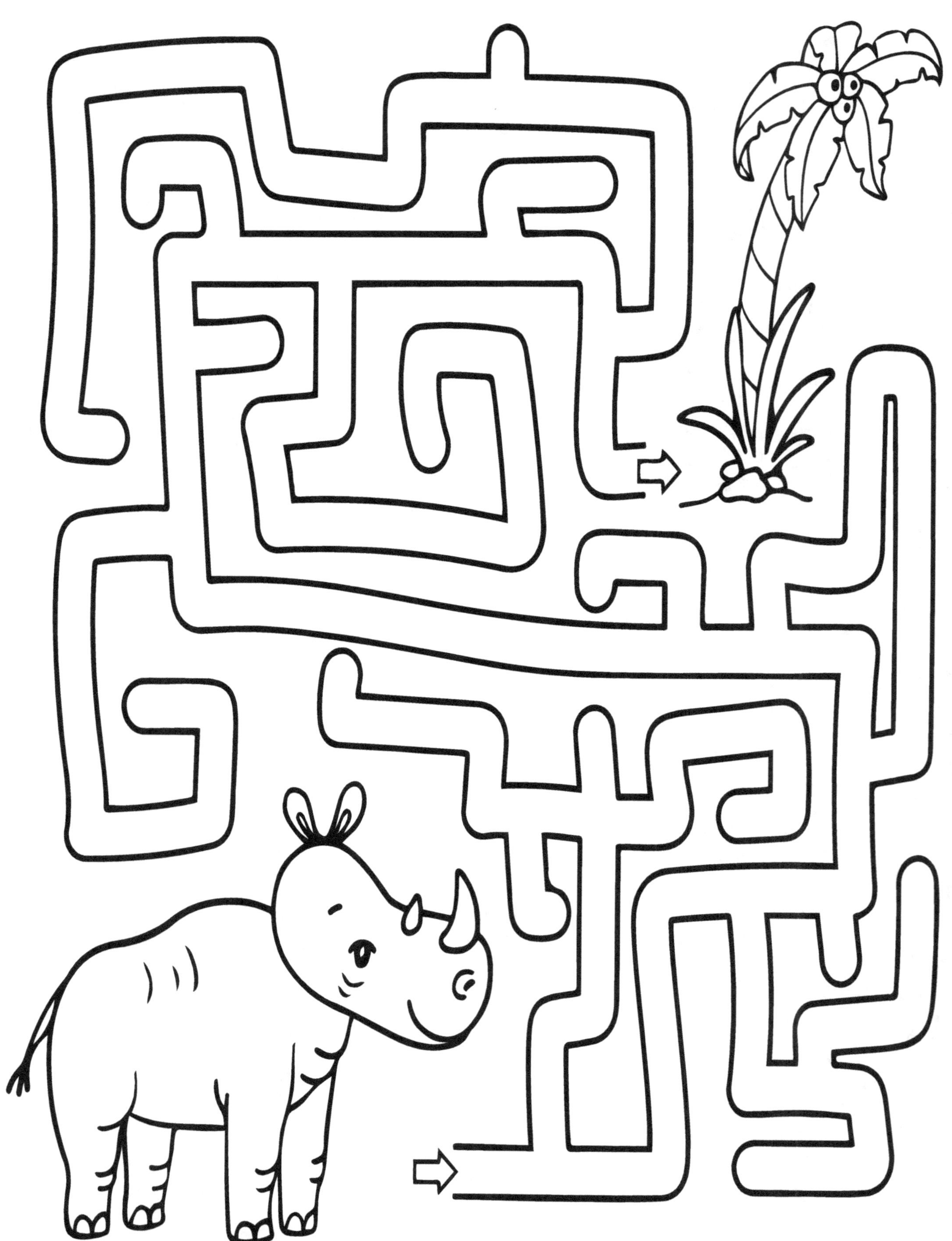

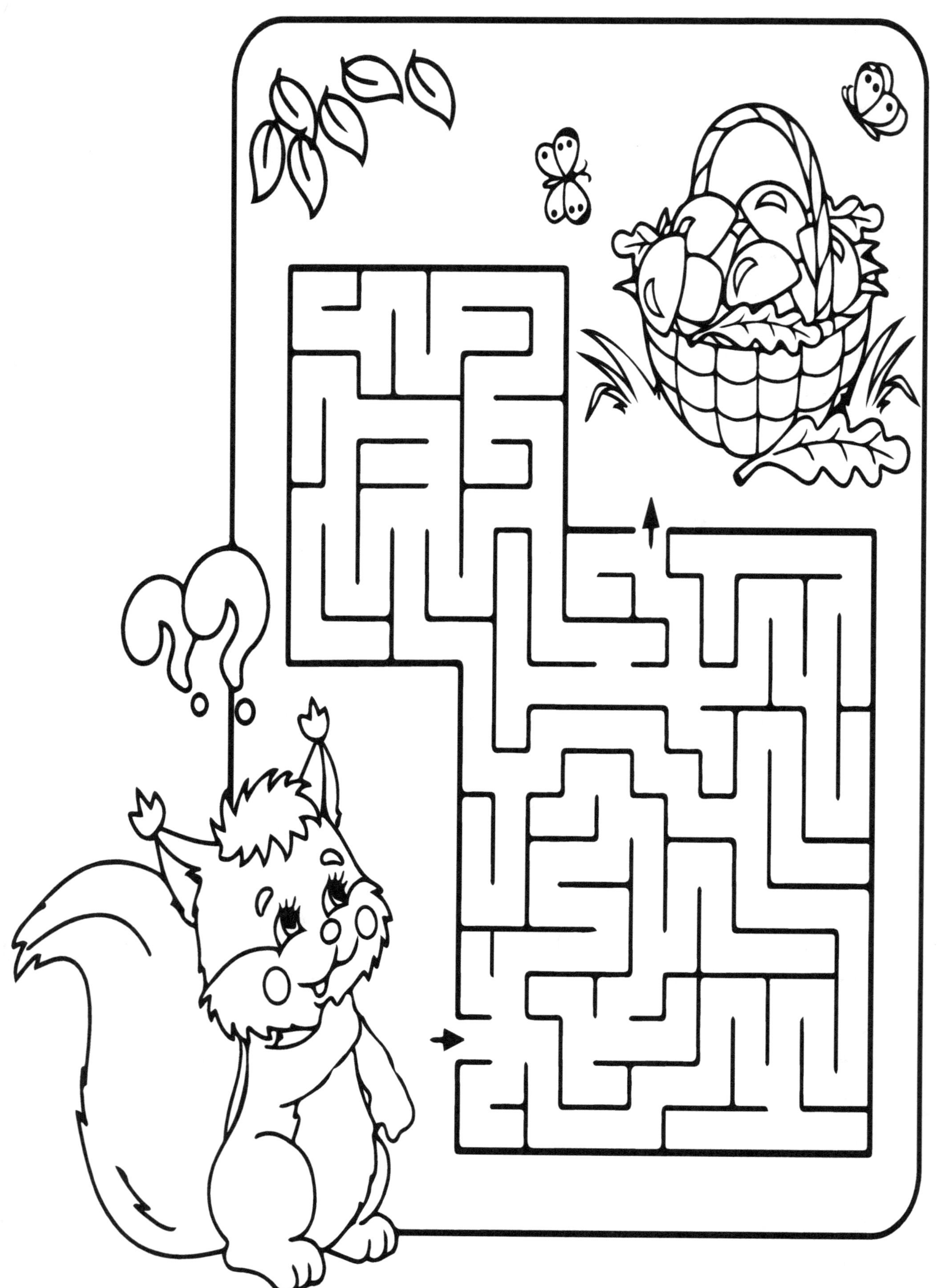

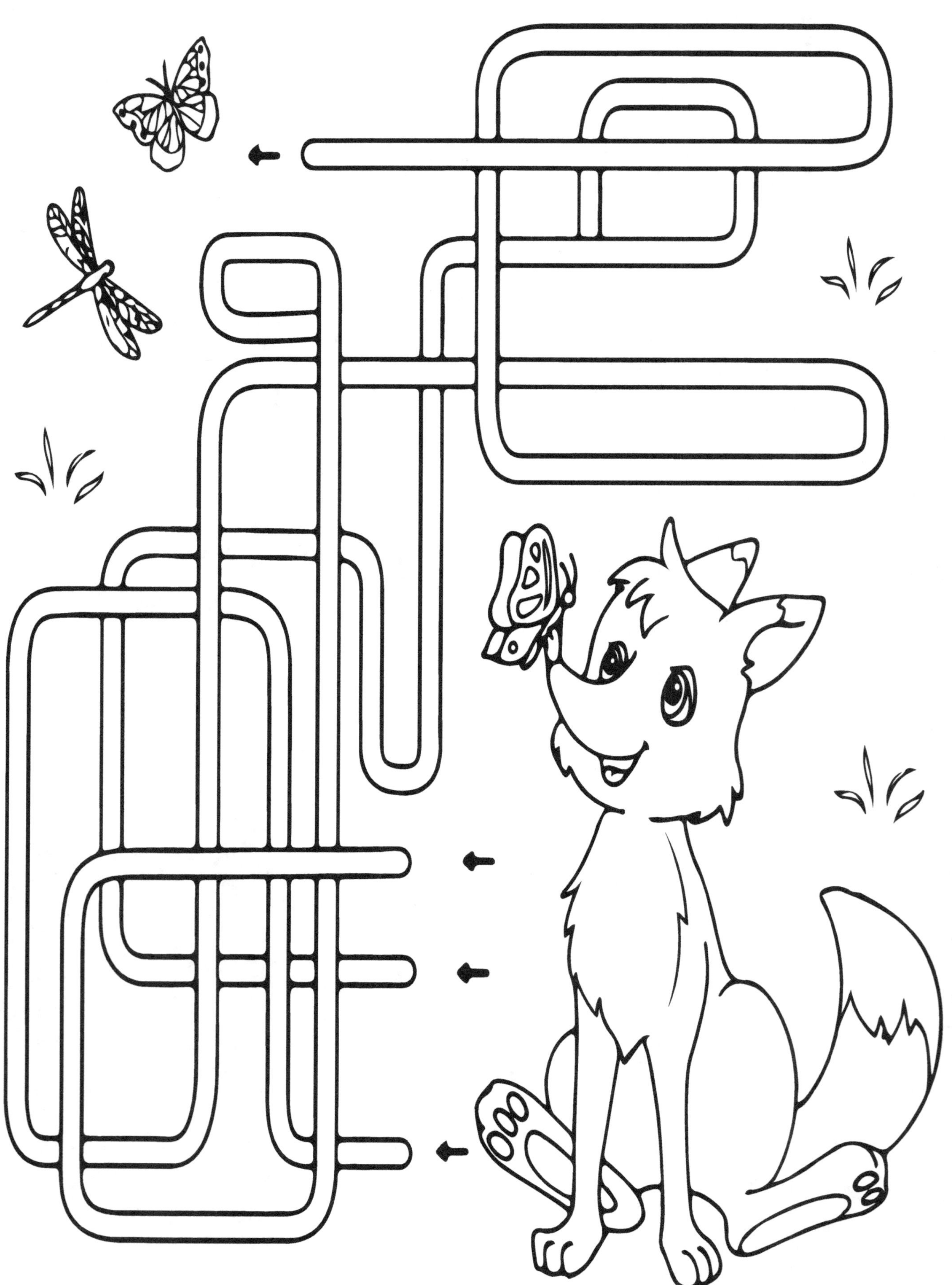

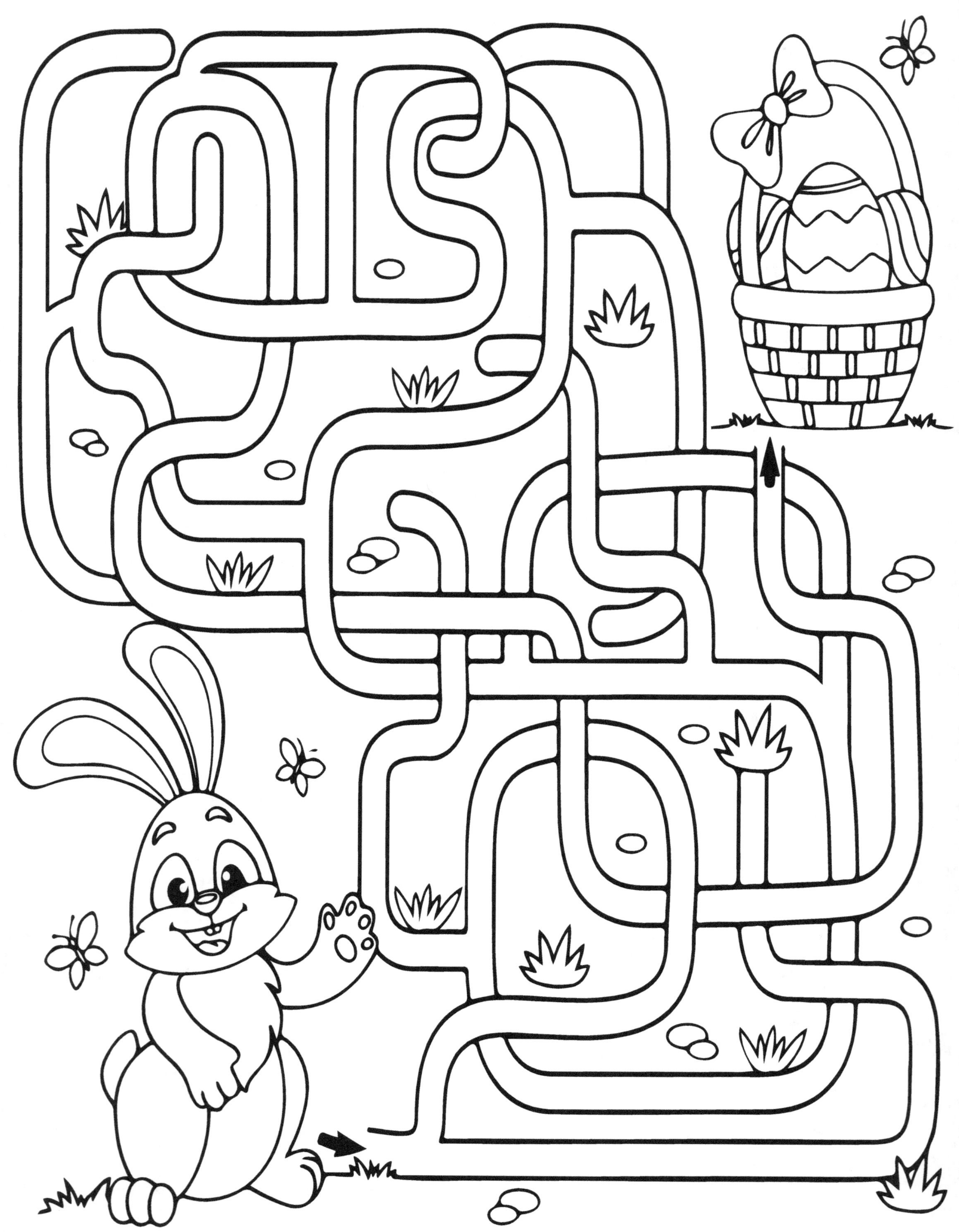

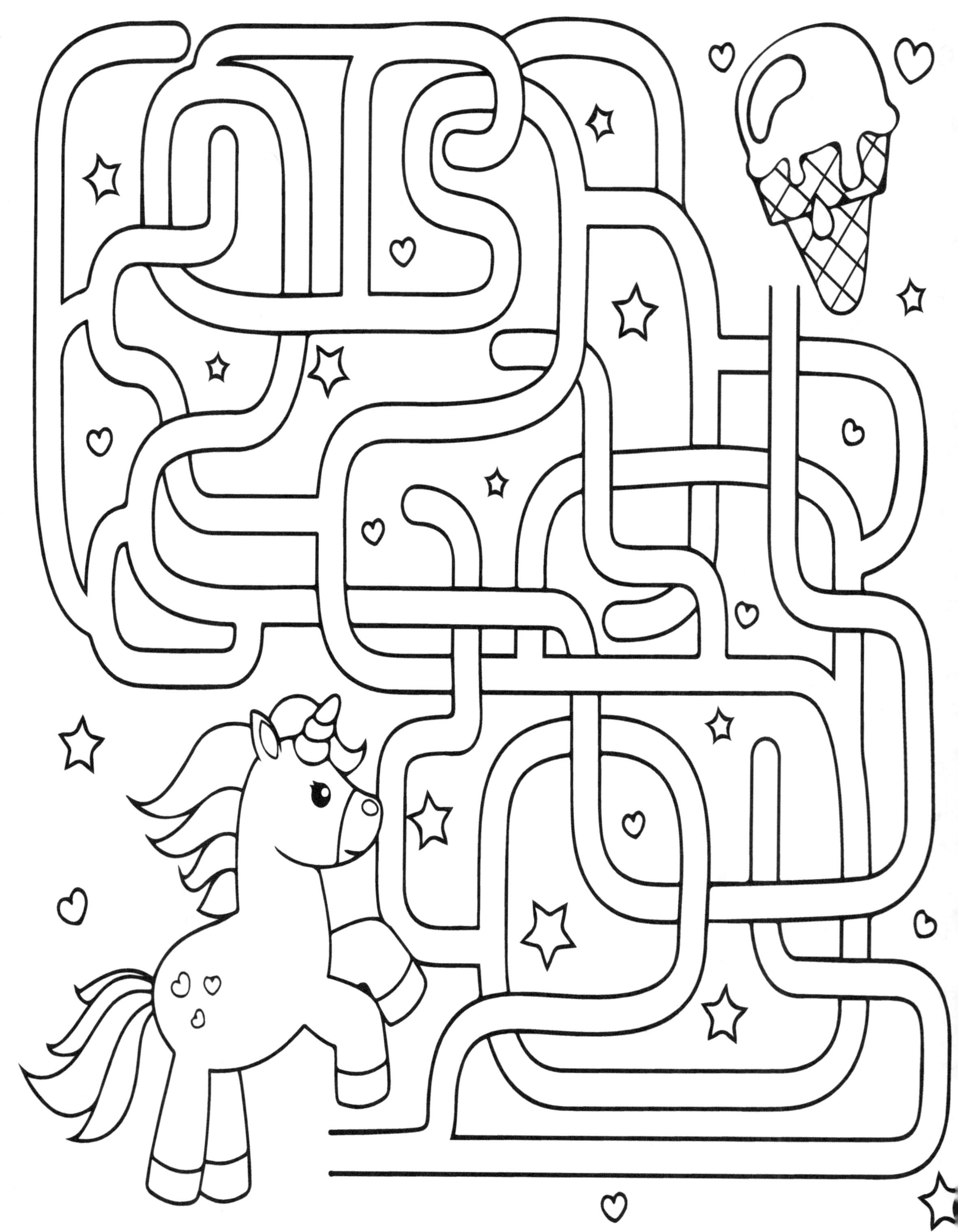